Uniforms and Equipment of U.S. Army Infantry, LRRPs, and Rangers in Vietnam 1965-1971

Uniforms and Equipment of U.S. Army Infantry, LRRPs, and Rangers in Vietnam
1965-1971

Paul W. Miraldi

Schiffer Military History
Atglen, PA

ACKNOWLEDGMENTS

This book is the result of many individuals who gave their time and help willingly and freely, and without their assistance this book could not have been completed!

The following are those who deserve a special thanks and who made the effort possible: Kevin Lyles, Eric Halsey, Main Photographer, Matthew J. Dias, Photographer, Steve Nelson, Tim Newark; Publisher "Military Illustrate", Reynold Cindrich, Tom McConnel, CSM Mike Martin, Dave George and Kaiser Bills, Nick Friedrich, Jeff Warner, Arik Greenberg, Mr. And Mrs. Greenberg, Larry Martin, Ben Singer, Eric Martin, Justin Atwood, J.L. Hansen, Larry Sutherland, Kirk Skaggs, Dan Spear, Glen Craigie, Russel Nakaegi, Tom Jones, Sam Lee, John Lu, Kurt Wheeler, A.J. Allen, Jon Jones, Frank G. Benns; Ranger Co. C, Gary Linderer, Mike O'Conner, Tom Newbauer, Lt. Mandrigal, Jack Applegate, Owen Thorton, Bernie Sahadi, Bob Chatt, Jay Camp, Dick Samms, The wonderful Kodak professionals at Target one hour film developing center—Andra Brannon, Justin Morales, Nicole Smith, and Crisha Brannon—Chino, Ca, Mr. Clay Hess, Mr. Teft, Mr. Scherff, Ray and Ron Torres, Ed Davies, Gary McDonnald, Jeff Lassiter, Pete V. Garcia, Jason Kimes, Brad Rettele, Sgt. Donald Glover; 25th Infantry, First Sgt. Minor Swackhammer, Paul Easter, Jeff Englert, Paul and Gary Hertig, Bill Tranzow, and my wife Amber.

This Book is dedicated to everyone who served in the 11(B) series (Infantry) Queen of Battle; Follow Me! Wartime and Peacetime, and especially to those who wore this stuff for real! In addition, "Iron Mike."

Book Design by Ian Robertson.

Library of Congress Control Number: 99-65343

Printed in China.
ISBN: 978-0-7643-0958-7

We are interested in hearing from authors with book ideas on related topics.

Published by Schiffer Publishing, Ltd.
4880 Lower Valley Road
Atglen, PA 19310
Phone: (610) 593-1777;
Fax: (610) 593-2002
E-mail: Info@schifferbooks.com
Web: www.schifferbooks.com

For our complete selection of fine books on this and related subjects, please visit our website at www.schifferbooks.com. You may also write for a free catalog.

Schiffer Publishing's titles are available at special discounts for bulk purchases for sales promotions or premiums. Special editions, including personalized covers, corporate imprints, and excerpts, can be created in large quantities for special needs. For more information, contact the publisher.

We are always looking for people to write books on new and related subjects. If you have an idea for a book, please contact us at proposals@schifferbooks.com.

Contents

Foreword

I met Paul in his natural environment—a gunshow—some years back, and we have shared our information and enthusiasm ever since.

I have watched as Paul has doggedly amassed what must surely be the finest collection of Vietnam related militaria in the U.S. As his collection has grown, so too has his stature in the hobby, and he has recently published several concise articles in the trade press.

Over the past decade, Paul has devoted his time, energy, and last, but certainly not least, his finances, to the study of the Vietnam era, which has in turn resulted in the publication of this book. Collectors new to the hobby are probably not aware how much they owe to enthusiasts like Paul. As a result of his hard work they certainly have it a whole lot easier than he or I did when we first started our collections with precious little information to guide us. This is definitely the book collectors have been waiting for.

Kevin Lyles
Artist and Author

Foreword

I have known the author, Paul Miraldi, for over 10 years, and in that time he has never stopped asking me questions. We have discussed every detail I could remeber about equipment, opperations, and insignia. He has detailed research on all "Special Operation" units, such as Rangers, and has compared them with other information he has obtained from other Veterans. Paul Miraldi has been very articulate with attention to detail on every aspect of uniforms, equipment, and insignia. He has interviewed, corresponded, and spoken to many other veterans that I know of in the LRRP, Ranger, and Infantry fields, and has compiled all this information into this informative book. His concern is to correctly document LRRP, Ranger, and Infantry opperations, and make them as accurate as possible. Paul's knowledge on these subjects has been demonstrated through his several previous publicated articles dealing with the subject matter. I know that collectors and historians will definitely want this book in their libraries.

Frank D. Benns
Co. C (ABN) 75th Infantry, RANGERS
3rd Platoon
RVN 1970-1971

Introduction

The sole purpose of this book is to accurately show the appearance of U.S Army Infantry troops, along with their uniforms, equipment, and personal items carried during the Vietnam War. This book is the first in a series I hope to publish in the coming years dedicated to the appearance of the fighting man during the Vietnam War. This book is the product of years of exhausting research, trials, and errors, along with extensive buying of uniforms and gear, many hours on the phone to Kevin Lyles, Author, in England, correspondence by mail, looking at thousands of photos and books, talking and meeting with Vets, as well as comparing notes with other collectors throughout the U.S. Another name that needs to be mentioned is by all means the Guru of Vietnam Uniforms and Equipment, Mr. Shelby Stanton, literally the Godfather of Uniform Histories! Without Mr. Stanton's outstanding research and his books, U.S. Army Uniforms of the Vietnam War and U.S. Army Uniforms of the Cold War, 1948-1973, this book would not have been possible, and many of us would still be in the dark about uniforms and equipment. Subsequently, Kevin Lyles' book, Vietnam: U.S. Uniforms in Color Photographs, and his book on Infantry with hundreds of original unpublished photos is a must, and without it and Kevin's help this book could not have been made possible.

The chapters are divided into years, and the figures are presented in chronological sequence so that the gradual development of uniforms, equipment, and weapons can be traced from year to year. In this way, it is possible to note at a glance when specific items were introduced into service. Each chapter will show the development of the items that were available, with close ups to further help the historian, collector, museum staff, etc., identify future items or items they may already have. One may also note that some chapters are longer than others are, and some units may be represented in greater numbers than others. Please do not think this is a bias on the part of the author; certain units' uniforms were harder to obtain over the years and did not make it into my collection, as well as unit histories, but rest assured that the next book will cover more of the units not represented in this volume. Due to time restraints and lack of items, many units were not covered fully.

The "scope" of the book has been limited to those Divisions that are listed as being Infantry, Airborne Infantry, Airmobile Infantry, LRRP, or Rangers. Other units, such as Engineers, M.P.s, armor, and artillery will hopefully be covered in future titles in this series. There are several medics portrayed and re-created in this volume, but considering that they endured the same hardships and did everything the "Grunts" did, if not more, I can't think of one grunt that would have any problem with medics being in a book about Infantry and Rangers. Besides, the Medics were as important a part of any Infantry platoon as the RTO, Platoon leader, or rifleman!

The research for this book started 18 years ago, when as a teenager my friends and I were fascinated with the armed forces, the Army and Marine corps, in particular. We would spend weekends organized into teams and wage war on each other throughout the many vacant fields, lots, and even the housing track of condominiums where I lived in Glendora/San Dimas in Southern California. Of course, we had to have the proper uniform for our "Wargames," and many of the other kids who had been doing this longer than me already had complete sets of camouflage, gear, boots, and uniforms, as well as fake M-16 rifles. Guys with only particle uniforms, foreign uniforms, or tennis shoes were not allowed to play, or if they were had only a minor role in the battle! This convinced me to do research on the units we as kids were "portraying," and to spend all week saving money and going to every swap meet, garage sale, or Military surplus store that the bus line went by or that was reachable by bike. Once I was able to put together a complete uniform of a modern solider in the Army I began to buy books on Vietnam. It was my goal, and later, obsession, to have a uniform(s) portraying Vietnam era soldiers. A friend of mine, Steve Nelson, who I consider my mentor for collecting, was a year older and much more knowledgeable about Vietnam. Steve already had a huge collection of uniforms, gear, and equipment, as well as WWII American, Japanese, and German items. I remember going to his house, which is where we all usually met, and being in total awe of everything he had. His home was like a small museum, and we kids would all jockey for his attention by whatever new item we had picked up or some new information we had gathered over the week.

Finally, as I got older and grew out of "playing" war and joined the U.S. Army, I realized this stuff was getting harder and harder to find and that it needed to be preserved and documented for further generations. However, at the time, there were no books dedicated to U.S. Uniforms in Vietnam. There were a few, but they were so horrible and incorrect that they are not worth mentioning here! Any information I could find was old Dept. of the Army

Field Manuals on uniforms. FMs like 21-15 Care And Use Of Individual Clothing and Equipment Aug, 1961, was very helpful. By this time I had compiled a large collection of M1956 gear, and pieces of the M1967 gear without really knowing what it was. Not until Shelby Stanton's first book came out in 1988 could I finally see what I actually had and what it was called. Now I was armed with the power, and once I got out of the Army, I was back in So Cal and all its Gun Shows and Militaria shows, where I met other collectors, like R.C. Cindrich and Tom McConnel, who helped me even more. In 1992 I attempted to submit a manuscript on Uniforms and Equipment to a publisher in England, who flatly refused and told me not to attempt to contact them again. This led me to do more research and devote more time and effort to getting my book completed. In 1996, Kevin Lyles helped get me a job writing articles on "Elite" Forces for an English Publication called Military Illustrated. I contacted Schiffer Publishing, Ltd. in November of 1997, they sent Bob Biondi out to meet with me, and I soon had a contract. Now, almost 10 years after I started, I have finally written this Schiffer Book, which culminates all of the information I have gathered on the history of Uniforms, gear, and equipment.

1

1965

2d Battalion of the 502d Infantry (Airborne)
1st Brigade, 101st Airborne Division
An Khe, Operation "Highland," 1965
Rifleman

"When the 1st Brigade of the 101st arrived in Vietnam, Col. James S. Timothy was given orders to open up the stretch of highway 19 between Qui Nhon on the coast and the inland town of An Khe. This clearing operation was designed to permit the 1st Cavalry Div. (Airmobile) to deploy peacefully to An Khe one month later. These paratroopers moved to An Khe and began Operation HIGHLAND. The sweep proceeded smoothly, and the operation concluded without incident. However, a V.C. main force battalion of the 2d NVA Regiment had been reported in the Song Con River valley to the north of An Khe Pass, and Col. Timothy wanted

Front View of 101st Airborne.

Back View showing minimal gear.

Close up showing the paratrooper's mid section. Note the hand grenades in the rifle bandoleer. This is also a good shot of the WWII hand axe.

Close up showing early 1962 dated sewing kit.

a crack at it. On Sept 18, 1965, he set Operation GIBRALTER into motion. The ground arm of the operation was to be a mechanized column, which would move north beside the Song Con River. The Airmobile force consisted of the 2d Battalion, 502nd Infantry (Airborne), under Lt. Col. Wilfrid K. G. Smith. It was to air-assault into the jungle highlands near An Ninh, consolidate its landing zone, then push the VC into the advancing armor of the other task force."[1]

"The Textile research conducted during the Korean War led to the development of more durable cotton material with the same weight as the herringbone twill fabric. During 1952, cotton sateen fabric was manufactured in Olive green shade 107 and used to produce the new utility jacket and trousers."[2] "The U.S. Army used the official designation "utility" for this uniform, which was consistent with the terminology of other services. The utility, or 'fatigues,' were intended to be loose fitting, although the shirt was normally worn tucked into the trousers and the trouser bloused when wearing combat boots. Army soldiers continued to call these fatigues because of the fatiguing duty performed while wearing them."[3] The first model OG 107 sateen shirt worn here came with flat, brown buttons. Trousers also featured the flat brown buttons and were worn with a black web trouser belt with a brass roller buckle.

Above his left pocket is the "U.S. Army distinctive tape, first authorized 27 Oct. 1953. The woven label has golden yellow block lettering on a black background. A nametape was added by local unit directives above the right pocket and contained the soldier's last name, first initial. Early name tapes were often in branch colors, but most were made of white engineer tape with black lettering."[4] Above the U.S. ARMY strip is a pair of basic Airborne wings. On the left sleeve he wears his Division's Shoulder Sleeve Insignia (SSI), 101st Airborne's Screaming Eagle, and his rank, Spc. 4.

Army web gear is shown here in typical fashion. A cotton H-harness is connected to a pistol belt, with two "universal pouches," sometimes mistakenly referred to as M-14 pouches, and one canteen and cover. The canteen cover, like the rest of the components of the M1956 gear, is made of cotton duck in OD number 7. It is lined with grey wool felt, which when wet is designed to keep the water in the 1-quart canteen cool. The two "Universal, small arms pouches, were designed to carry a wide variety of magazines. It could hold two B.A.R. magazines, one folded bandoleer of M-1, six M-1 clips, or four 30 round carbine magazines. The pouch closed with a quick release fastener, by putting a web tab through a billet sewn on the front of the pouch. The case also featured a back-supporting strap that could be extended and snapped to the front of the suspenders, which kept the pouch from hanging forward when loaded with ammo. Grenades could be secured on either side by means of a strap and slots."[5] Each soldier was usually issued two of these pouches. Worn on the left side of his pistol belt is the entrenching tool, or E-tool, in its cover. The cover is also made of cotton duck material in OD shade 7. The carrier attaches to the pistol belt with two interlocking slide

Close up showing the kit open and the contents minus the needles. The date is at the top—1962.

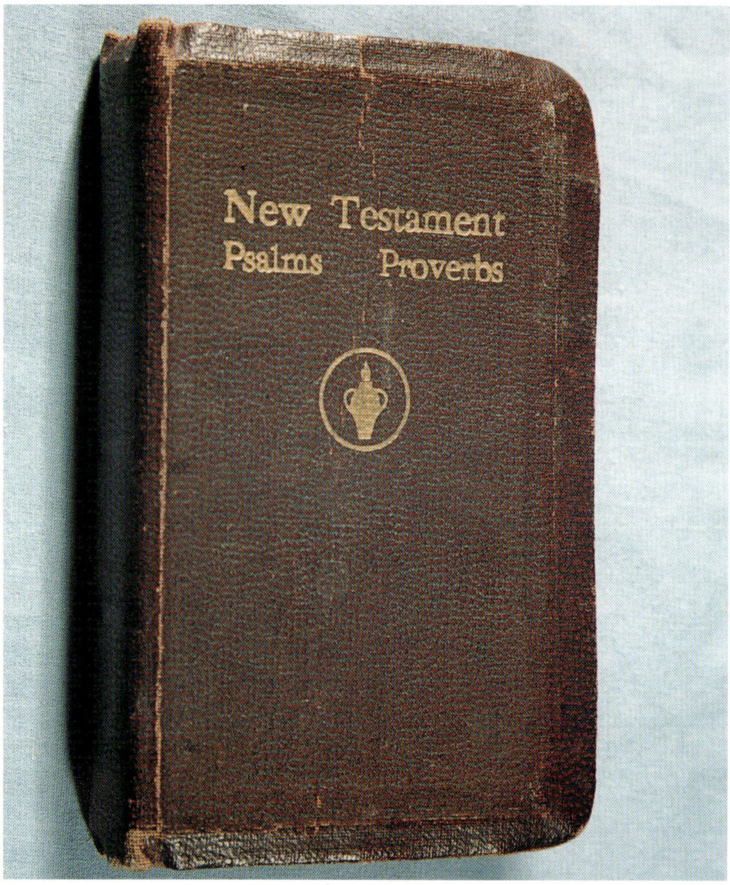

Close up of early New Testament soldier's Bible.

Company B, 1st Battalion, 7th Cavalry,
1st Cavalry Division
Ia Drang Valley, Chu Prong Massif
LZ X-Ray, 14 November 1965.
RTO

"In March 1965, the decision was made to convert the 11th Air Assault Division (Test) to a full-fledged member of the Army structure. It was decided that the new division would carry the colors of the 1st Cavalry Division, which was then deployed in South Korea. On 1 July 1965 the 1st Cavalry Division (Airmobile) was officially activated, and the first full division was to arrive in Vietnam on 11 September 1965. Mag.Gen. Harry W.O. Kinnards's 1st Cavalry Div. was providing traffic security along Highway 19 with both heliborne and dismounted sweeps, when it was called into action as a result of the North Vietnamese Army attacks against Plei Me, south of Pleiku. The division would call it Operation Silver Bayonet, but its Airmobile actions over the fifteen hundred square mile battlefield of western South Vietnam would be registered in military history as the "Ia Drang Valley" campaign."[6]

This "First Team" RTO wears the 1st pattern Tropical Combat uniform. On his left sleeve is the SSI of the 1st Cavalry Div., along with full color U.S. Army and name tapes above his two breast pockets. Underneath, he wears a standard white cotton T-shirt, although much of the 1st Cav. dyed these green before deploying to South East Asia. On his back, the RTO carries the new

keepers on the rear. A leather reinforcement tab and web strap on the front of the carrier is provided to receive the double hook fastener of the bayonet or bayonet knife scabbard. This Airborne troop has decided to carry the Army hatchet instead of the bayonet on his E-tool carrier. On the right side of his H-harness he carries his angle head flashlight. Worn across his chest, oddly enough, is an M-16 cotton bandoleer, filled with 6 M27 handgrenades, along with an early model Claymore bag with Claymore mine. An early M-16 rifle is carried with two twenty round magazines taped end to end for rapid reloading, which if you note has already been done, because he now has the empty one on the bottom. Helmet is the standard M-1 helmet with the paratrooper helmet liner.

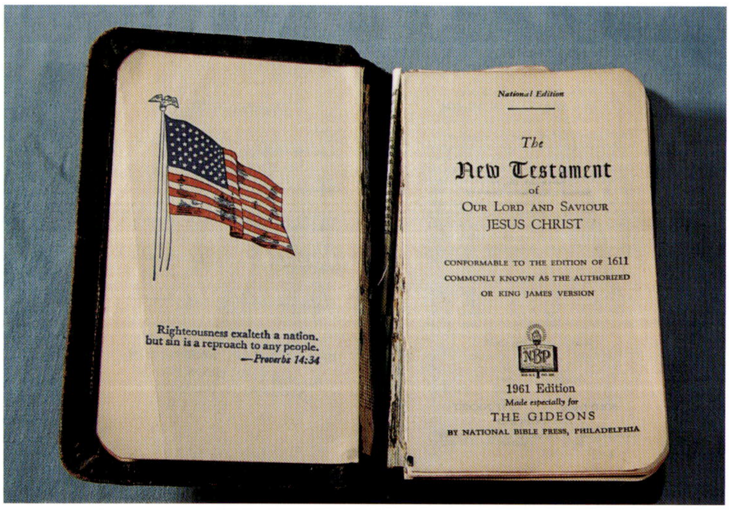

Close up showing the Bible opened, note the date, 1961.

Full Figure shot of 1st Cavalry R.T.O.

Left: *R.T.O. Utilizing new PRC 25 radio. This shot provides a good view of both the 1st Cav. SSI and the bayonet fixed to his M16 rifle.* Right: *Full rear shot showing the PRC 25 on its carrier.*

Close up showing side view of E-tool and carrier and spare parts bag. Note the WWII era 1st Cav. SSI.

Close up showing poncho secured under radio.

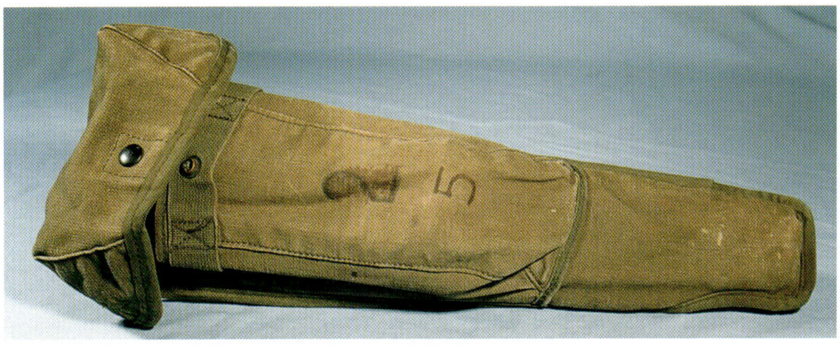

Close up of spare parts bag for the RTO's PRC-25

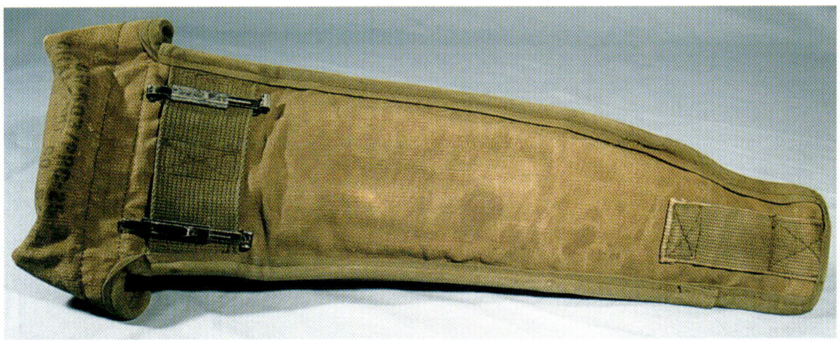

Close up of backside of spare parts bag.

Close up showing LBE and exposed button shirt. Note the "Skillcraft" pen and plastic spoon.

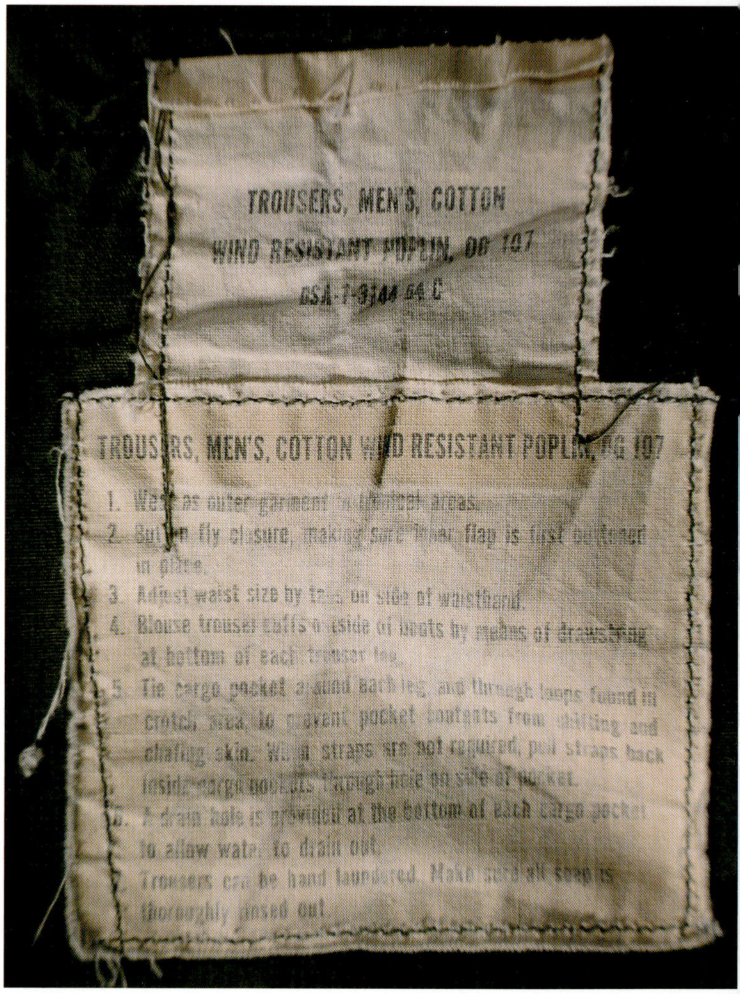

Close up of two large tags inside the 1st model Trousers, Man's, Cotton, Wind Resistant, Poplin, OG 107.

Close up showing the Tay Coat, Mans, Combat, Tropical. Note the 1964 date. DSA-1-2961-64-C

Close up showing the button fly and three tags inside 1st model exposed button trousers.

Close up showing white tag inside the tongue of the early 1964-65 pattern jungle boots. By late 1965, this tag would be replaced, and the new ankle support would be added by Dec. 1965.

Close up of top/inside of left jungle boot. Note the size 10 R followed by the manufacture date; 9 65.

AN/PRC-25 FM Radio with its own web carrying assembly. The 1st Cavalry was one of the first units deployed to South East Asia to receive this radio. Most units, like the 25th Infantry and U.S. Marine Corps, had to make due with the older, unreliable AN/PRC-10. The spares bag, attached to the left side of the radio by a D-ring, contained the sectional long-range antenna with a flexible base, along with an additional spare handset. Beneath the radio, the RTO has secured his poncho with 550 cord. By late 1966 or early 1967, the AN/PRC-25 would replace the AN/PRC-10 in most U.S. Army line units. In 1962, a new designed boot was issued, which was eight and a half inches tall and no longer featured the toe cap. This new boot was later adopted by both the U.S. Army and Marine Corps, and was part of a standardization of supply in both forces. This new boot would take on the nickname "McNamara" boots, after Sec. of Defense Robert McNamara.

Web gear consists of two universal small arms cases, with one M-26 grenade, a compass pouch, and one M18 smoke grenade. On his left hip is the E-tool carrier and the M1951 combination tool, along with the M-7 bayonet. The M-1 Steel helmet with the Mitchel leaf Pattern cover was the standard headgear for line troops in combat at this time.

Weapon is the new AR-15, better known as the M-16 rifle in 5.56 with the M7 bayonet affixed. The 1st Cavalry was one of the first Army units to receive these new, lightweight rifles.

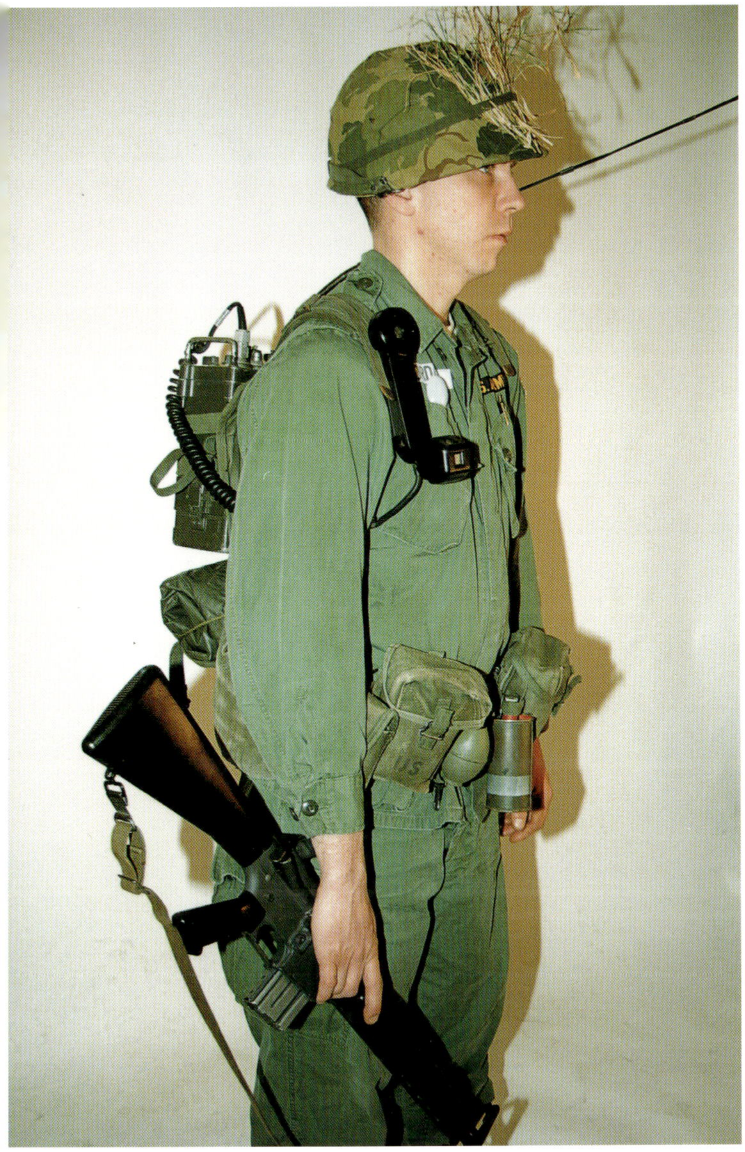

Right side of Cav. Trooper.

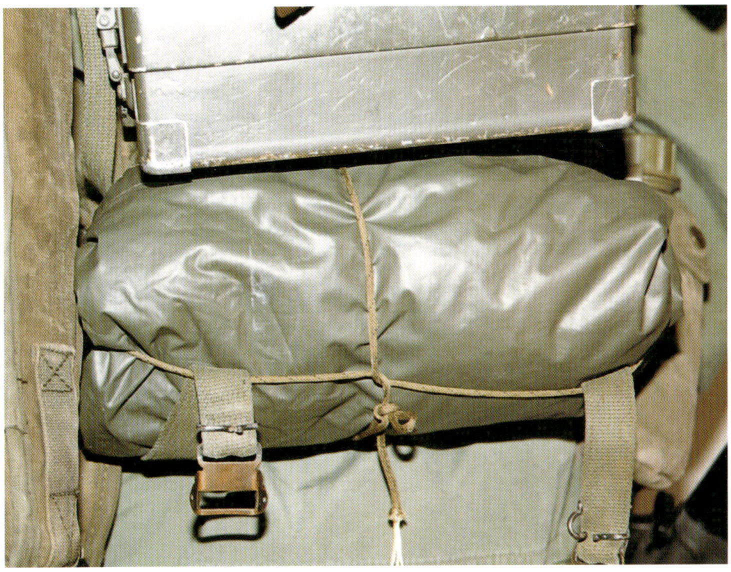

Close up showing poncho tied to Radio frame, note the 550 cord.

Full front view of 1st Cavalry Platoon Sgt.

Right side of Platoon Sgt. Note the civilian knife on his belt.

5th Battalion, 7th Cavalry,
1st Cavalry Division
LZ Albany, 1965
Platoon Sergeant

The uniform worn here is another example of the OG 107 utility uniform, which was first produced in 1952. The fatigue shirt has two upper patch pockets with rectangular buttoned flaps each secured with a single button. The matching cotton utility trousers have two front and two rear pockets, each secured with a button flap, and side button take-up tabs on the waist. A full color 1st Cavalry patch is worn on his left shoulder, while on his combat side, he wears a full color 7th Infantry "Bayonet" Division

Close up showing his web gear. Note the white plastic C-rat spoon in the universal pouch.

Close up showing his PRC-6 radio secured in his M1956 butt pack. This also provides a good view of the two 1qt canteens and covers.

Good view of 1st Cav. Patch on his left sleeve, and his chow sock.

Platoon Sgt. Inspecting his new trophy, a captured SKS rifle.

patch, showing a combat tour in Korea. Below that is a set of E-7 stripes, Sgt. First class. Worn above his Black and Gold U.S. Army strip is a pin back metal C.I.B. Items worn on his LBE consist of the M1956 cotton H-suspenders with a single D-ring and his "chow sock" attached to the left side. This was nothing more than an ordinary OD green boot sock filled with the desired amount of C-ration cans for a day or more. On his M1956 pistol belt he has two universal pouches with a total of three M26 grenades and a single white plastic C-rat spoon, his "M1951 combination entrenching tool, or E-tool, in its M1956 carrier, which featured a leather attachment tab and web strap to secure the M7 bayonet in its M8A1 scabbard."[7] On his right side he carries two, 1qt canteens with their M1956 carriers, one is affixed to the belt, while the other is secured to his M1956 Combat Field pack, or "Butt Pack," which was designed for mobile armored infantry operations and supported by his suspenders. Inside the flap, he has secured his AN/PRC 6 "handi-talkie" Korean War era radio, which features a flexible tape antenna and a telephone style hand microphone, along with extra socks, grenades, rations, and magazines. Pre-1962 Black leather combat boots are worn here featuring the "old style" toe-cap, which was recently done away with. Weapon is the newly issued and recently "battle tested" M-16 rifle, with double 20 round magazines taped end to end for rapid reloading, along with the M7 bayonet attached for close quarter fighting. In his other hand he carries an SKS rifle as a souvenir of the battle, which by the time he gets back to Camp Holloway will be in the possession of some R.E.M.F. officer.

Close up showing Platoon Sgt.'s Shirt. Note the pin on CIB. And the man's name, ironically, is "Armstrong."

ARMY DIGEST: Dated September, 1965.

1st Battalion, 503d Infantry (Airborne),
173rd Airborne Brigade
Vung Tau, 1965
Rifleman

"Brigadier General Ellis W. Williamson's 173d Airborne Brigade on Okinawa was the Army's own compact, two-fisted response force for the western Pacific, designed to drop in under canopies of silk and seize immediate objectives until something bigger could reinforce the situation. Its two fists were the 1st and 2d Battalions of the 503d Infantry (Airborne), which was the first parachute infantry regiment into the Pacific during WWII. The paratroopers arrived in Vietnam on May 5, and were under the impression that Vietnam was temporary duty and that another airborne brigade from the states would replace them soon. The brigade of the 173d was the first Army ground combat unit to arrive in S. Vietnam. It was H.Q. at Bien Hoa, outside Saigon where it expected to be used as a countrywide fire brigade. Instead, one battalion was detained to pull guard duty at Vung Tau the landing point for Army units arriving by sea, and its other battalion dug in around the Bien Hoa air base as security."[8]

Full front View of 503d Paratrooper.

Good right side of 173d paratrooper loading his new M16 rifle. Note from this angle you can see the early 1st model 2qt canteen with cover.

Close up of early 1st model (experimental) 2qt canteen and cover.

Backside of cover. Some of these are dated 1962. Note the lack of "slide keepers" for attaching the cover to the web belt or rucksack. The strap can be adjusted, but cannot be removed.

"The Tropical Combat uniform, or "Jungle Fatigues," was the primary field uniform in Vietnam after 1963. This uniform was a rare example of Army clothing that combined functional practicality with comfort and an attractive design. The quick drying coat and trousers were made of a tightly woven lightweight twill cotton fabric. The loose fitting garments promoted body and heat ventilation and moisture dissipation. The coat was designed to be worn outside the trousers, and sleeves were allowed to be rolled up. In fact, it became mandatory to roll up the sleeves above the elbows neatly in military installations and rolled down while in the fields. The coat features two slanted chest pockets, which allowed soldiers ease in removal of items, and two lower bellow pockets. The shirt also incorporated shoulder loops, side button take up tabs, and an "inner gas flap." All buttons on the garment are exposed."[9] "The trousers also featured the 'exposed' buttons to match the shirt. They featured two rear pockets, two front pockets, and two large bellow cargo leg pockets. Inside the cargo pockets were two integral tie down straps much like the M1951 field trouser offered. Inside the left cargo pocket was a small one-button pocket that was designed to hold a small survival kit that was never satisfactorily developed or issued."[10]

Headgear worn underneath the M-1 helmet is the utility cap, which was a visor baseball style cap made out of polyester and

Close up of small tag inside the Coat, Man's, Combat Tropical. DSA-12397-63-C. shows the date is 1963, the first year the Tropical uniform was produced.

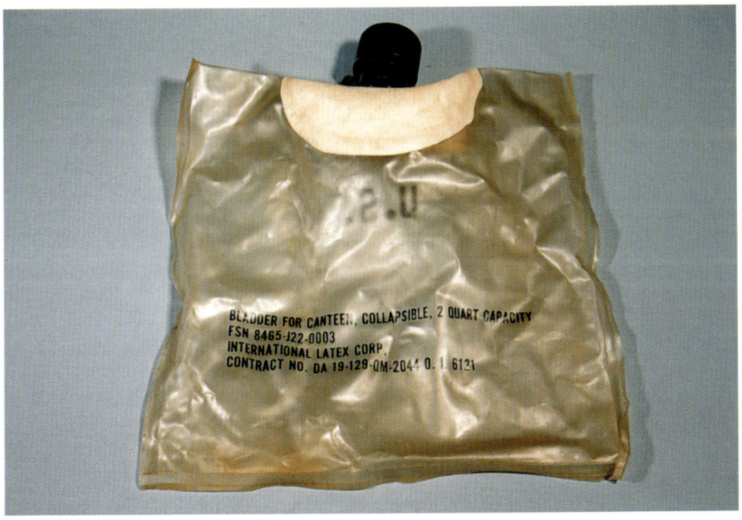

Close up showing the actual 2qt canteen.

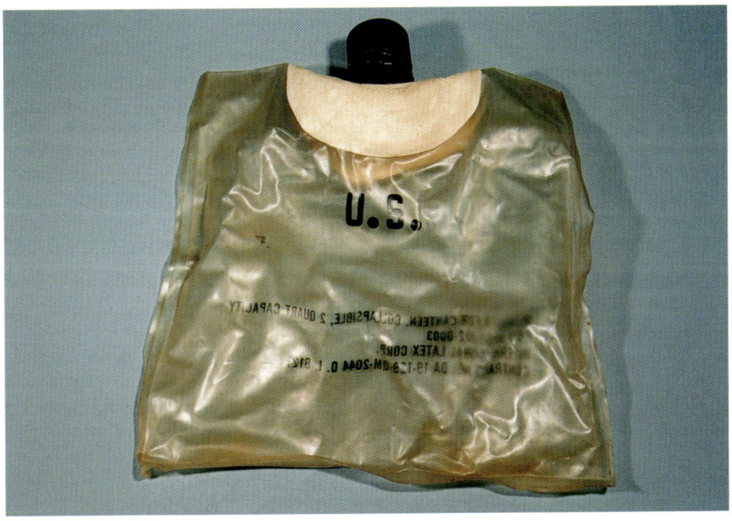

Close up of the front of the 2qt collapsible canteen.

Full left view provides a good look at his M17 mask, along with his E-tool and cover.

Close up showing the "Exposed Buttons" of the 1st model Tropical Jungle Fatigues. Note the lime green color of the two buttons on the pocket flap. The 1963 model had these lime green buttons. The next year, the buttons would be a flat "dull" green.

Close up showing the very rare bottle of "bug juice" with the paper label. This one is dated 1965.

Close up showing the early second model jungle boots with the Vibram soles and lacking the ankle reinforcements. (Arik Greenberg collection.)

Rear view showing an early version of the Lightweight rucksack, produced in 1963.

Close up of white cotton tag that appears in both boots in the tongue of the boot. Both the 1964 and 1965 production year had this tag. The tag shows these boots were produced in 1964, as is evident by the 64-E on the last line. (Arik Greenberg collection.)

Comparison of a WWII Angle head flashlight (Top) and a Vietnam era flashlight (Bottom).

Close up showing the small differences between the two flashlights. The WWII (Right), made by Ray-O-Vac, does not have the clip, while the Vietnam War era one features the clip. (Left).

Typical 1st model OG 107 cotton Sateen shirt. This is what most members of the Elite 173d wore when they arrived in Vietnam. It wouldn't be too long before they were outfitted with the new lightweight Jungle fatigues.

Left sleeve showing the two piece SSI of the 173d "Airborne," along with an E-2 chevron.

rayon gabardine cloth, dyed Olive Green army shade 106. The cap was first adopted in 1962 after a long search by the Army to replace the headgear of the Korean War era. Airborne units like the 173rd were allowed to wear their Airborne wings affixed to the regimental colored ovals, to instill "Esprit de Corps." Worn across his chest is the prototype first model 2-quart canteen with cover. These were developed in 1962 for Special Forces serving in South East Asia, and were based on a WWII design. They featured a nylon carrying case with an integrated sling that could be adjusted but not removed, and a large "belt loop" instead of the M1956 individual equipment slide lock keepers. The canteen itself had problems with sealing and leaked often, so a new design was developed. Boots are the new 2nd model DMS Tropical Combat Boot with Vibram soles, which were available in this style by 1964, having done away with the early leather reenforcement along the top and vertically up the heel.

Weapon is the M16 5.56 rifle with two twenty round magazines taped end to end.

Close up of pocket with basic airborne wings and an early U.S. Army strip.

2

1966

**1st Battalion, 18th Infantry,
1st Infantry Division, "Big Red One"
Bien Hoa, 1966
Automatic Rifleman**

"The 1st Battalion, 18th Infantry, under the command of Colonel Simmons 2d Brigade, landed at the port in Cam Ranh Bay on 11 July 1965. The remainder of the 1st Infantry Division and its remaining Brigades would arrive at Bien Hoa, Vietnam, on 2 October 1965."[11]

Front view of automatic rifleman. Note the front handgrip on the full automatic M14.

OG 107 cotton sateens are still worn here in 1966 by some unlucky units, such as the 18th. On his first model shirt he wears full color U.S. ARMY, white name strip, SPC. 4 rank, and a 1st Infantry SSI. Underneath is a white GI issue T-shirt. This soldier

U.S. paratroopers move out in the mountains northwest of Tuy Hoa, 254 miles from Saigon, as Operation "Harrison" is started. All three men visible wear the second model jungle fatigues devoid of any SSI of the 101ST. The soldier at the left carries a Thermite grenade on his left side secured to his H-harness. The soldier in the center carries a WWII "Pineapple" grenade on his pistol belt. Note the RTO in the back with the shotgun, the radio headset, and what appears to be a sleeping bag secured to his PRC/25. The soldier at far right that is barely visible is the medic, made evident by his medical backpack. 07 March 66

Rear view of automatic rifleman.

Full front view of 4th Infantry Division soldier, 1966.

Close up showing the M1961 buttpack and machete in its sheath.

wears the second model DMS boots, which like the first model lacked the ankle reenforcement strip, which would be incorporated in late 1965. The second model Tropical Combat Boot, DMS did away with the leather strip running up the Achilles' tendon, and the leather strip along the top of the boot, which is now reenforced with nylon. A new type of slip in spike resistant insole was available, which was strips of steel encased in plastic, but many soldiers decided not to utilize them due to the fact that when worn on long marches the insole got hot and caused unnecessary blisters. This style, the second model Tropical Combat Boot, or "Jungle boot," was the first one issued in any great numbers. There were several earlier variations without the DMS, but these were few and far between, and the "Jungle boot" is the true 2nd model that was adopted by both the Army and Marine Corps in 1965. Web gear consists of a cotton H-harness connected to a M1956 pistol belt. Four universal pouches are worn on his belt, each containing three 20 round magazines for his fully automatic M-14E3 model rifle. A basic rifle squad consists of the following: a squad leader (E6); two team leaders (E5), Alpha Team and Bravo Team; two automatic rifle men, one in each team; two grenadiers, each with an M-79; and two additional riflemen. The riflemen, grenadiers, and auto riflemen under the two sergeants (E5) would all be E-1 through E-4. The M14E3 would soon be replaced by the M16 rifle, in which the automatic rifleman would also have an

Full left side showing the 4th Inf. Div. SSI.

Full right side of 4th Inf. Div. Soldier.

Full rear view.

aluminum bi-pod. Connected on the back is the M1961 butt pack with three canteens with covers. Two contain the newer plastic canteen, and one M1910 metal canteen. The fully auto version of the M14 rifle carried here is the M14E3, which featured a pistol grip at the buttstock, an additional fold down polyurethane foregrip, an extra long "assault sling," and bi-pod legs. Two 20 round magazines are seen here taped together end to end for rapid reloading.

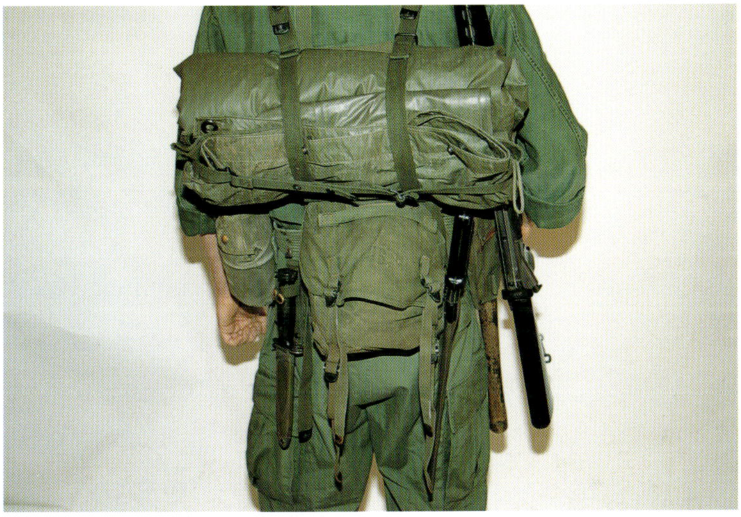

Close up of poncho/poncho liner secured in "spaghetti straps." Note the bayonet in the scabbard.

2nd Battalion, 8th Infantry (Mechanized), 4th Infantry Division "Operation Paul Revere IV," 1966 Rifleman

"The 4th Infantry Division was a good, solid Regular Army outfit with its men. For ten years, since 1956, it had been stationed at Ft. Lewis, at the southern end of Washington's Puget Sound region. There, in the woods, near Mt. Olympic near Tacoma, it had trained for atomic and mechanized warfare in a European theater. Its shoulder patch was of World War One vintage and featured four green ivy leaves. This design gained it the simple title 'Ivy Division,' which the troops fondly modified to the Poison Ivy Division."[12] "'Operation Paul Revere IV' was a continuing operation near the Cambodian border of Pleiku Province. It was conducted primarily by the 4th Infantry Division, along with elements of the 25th Infantry Division and the 1st Cavalry Division (Airmobile). 977 known enemy casualties were reported."[13]

This 4th Infantry Division soldier is lucky enough to have received the bottom half of the new Tropical combat uniform, which was not uncommon to see in 1966. Full color insignia is worn on the second model OG 107 to include an SSI of the 4th

Close up showing front of LBE. Note the M18 smoke and the first aid/compass pouch secured to the universal pouch, along with the brass roller buckle on his black web trouser belt.

Close up of early full color 4th Infantry Division SSI.

"Ivy" Division, E-4 SPC rank, U.S. Army, and name. Web gear consist of a M1956 pistol belt, with two universal pouches used to hold rounds for his M-16 rifle, two M-26 grenades, an M-6 bayonet in its M8A1 scabbard, and one canteen with its cover. Connected to the rear of the pistol belt is the larger "M1961 buttpack, which was quite a bit bigger, and featured a waterproof throat around the opening. Raising the flap and adjusting the web strap buckles could expand the compact size of the 9X9-inch compartment. Two bottom web straps were used to secure extra gear, such as a rolled poncho, underneath the pack. It also featured a row of eyelets for the attachment of the M1910 double hook fasteners. A M1942 machete in its sheath is secured to the right side of his buttpack."[14] "His poncho and poncho liner are connected to his suspenders via a complicated mess of straps known as the 'sleeping gear carrier,' but more commonly known as the 'Spaghetti straps.'"[15] His M-I helmet is worn with the green side out. Boots are the second model, which featured the Direct Molded Soles (DMS).

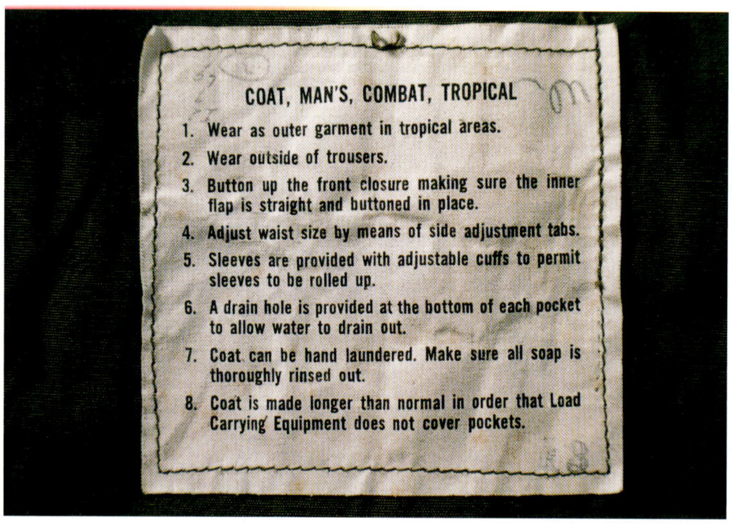

COAT, MAN'S, COMBAT, TROPICAL

1. Wear as outer garment in tropical areas.
2. Wear outside of trousers.
3. Button up the front closure making sure the inner flap is straight and buttoned in place.
4. Adjust waist size by means of side adjustment tabs.
5. Sleeves are provided with adjustable cuffs to permit sleeves to be rolled up.
6. A drain hole is provided at the bottom of each pocket to allow water to drain out.
7. Coat can be hand laundered. Make sure all soap is thoroughly rinsed out.
8. Coat is made longer than normal in order that Load Carrying Equipment does not cover pockets.

Close up of tag inside the 2nd model Coat, Combat, Tropical.

1st Battalion, 5th (Mechanized) Infantry,
25th Infantry Division
Michelin Rubber Plantation, 1966
RTO

This mechanized soldier from the "Tropic Lightning" wears the Army M1952 flak vest, which was standardized for U.S. Army ground troops at this time. This vest first saw action during the

Front view of 25th RTO.

Close up of sleeve. This V would be removed in the "rip-stop" uniform in a few years.

Close up button fly of 2nd model Trousers showing the instruction tag.

Korean War, and was worn by both U.S. and ARVN troops throughout the war. This soldier has also chosen to use the grenade hangers to keep a single M18 smoke grenade in a handy place. Inside his right pocket, he carries a private purchase knife, either sent over from home or purchased at the local PX.

Underneath his M1952 flak vest, he wears the second pattern tropical combat uniform, which featured covered buttons, but retained the shoulder loops and side take up tabs. On his second model shirt he wears a full color SSI of the 25th "Electric Strawberry." The second model trouser are also worn, which featured

Close up of shoulder loop on 2nd model Tropical shirt.

Close up showing the "button" take-up tab on the 2nd model trousers.

Right side of RTO.

Left side of 25th RTO. From this angle you can see the full color 25th SSI.

Rear view of "Tropic Lightning" soldier.

Backside showing PRC-10 radio.

covered buttons and integrated cargo straps in the large pockets."

Worn here are the new Tropical Combat boots, more commonly known as the "Jungle Boots," that were officially adopted in Jan. 1965. They featured a cotton/nylon upper, which were cool and quick drying, a cleated sole, and two-screened eyeholes for drainage. The design was so successful, that other than an added strip to reinforce the ankles, a slip in "spike protector" and a new anti-mud sole, the boot would remain unchanged and in service with the armed forces for 25 more years.

Seen here carried in its own canvas web carrying harness is the AN/PRC-10 FM Radio, along with the spare parts bag. The PRC-10 was still common to both the Army and the USMC in 1966, and was unreliable and not well suited for Vietnam's jungles and mountainous terrain. The PRC 10 would soon be replaced by the AN/PRC-25 in the coming months, although some units, such as the 1st Inf. Div. and the 1st Cav., arrived with the newer radios.

Close up showing the 2nd model 2qt canteen and cover.

Close up showing the AN/PRC-10 radio on its carrying assembly.

Close up showing the back of the cover; it reads "Cover, Canteen, Collapsible 2-Quart Capacity. NWSE 8465-889-3769."

Close up showing the actual canteen.

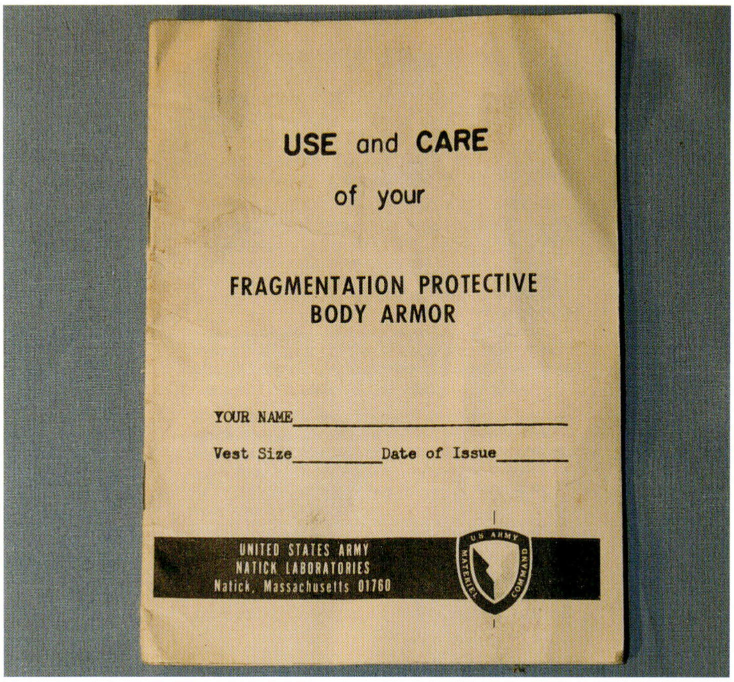

Close up of the manual that came with the flak vest.

Web gear consists of a M1956 pistol belt, two universal pouches, one M1956 canteen cover, and a newer 1-quart plastic canteen, which were first introduced to troops in 1963. On his left hip is a second model 2qt. Collapsible canteen, which became available in 1966 and consisted of a "square, molded vinyl bladder and an M1910 pattern cap with chain that was centered on the canteen body. The canteen cover lacked D-rings for a strap and could only be worn on the belt or in other awkward positions."[16] The Cotton H-harness is worn here over his M1952 flak vest.

Close up head shot shows the PRC-10 hand mike and a purple M18 smoke grenade.

2nd Battalion, 12th Cavalry,
1st Cavalry Division, "Operation Masher"/"White Wing"
Phung Du, 1966
Rifleman

"Maj. Gen Harry Kinnards 1st Cavalry Division (Airmobile), stationed at Camp Radcliff outside An Khe, was ordered to clear four important valleys located along the coastal plains of northeastern Bihn Dihn Province. Reinforced by the ARVN Airborne Brigade, 22nd ARVN Division, and the 1st Regiment of the Korean Capital Division, Col. Harold G. Moore, Jr.'s 3d Brigade entered combat there on Jan. 25th. It was followed by the 2d and later 1st brigades. On Feb. 4, Operation 'MASHER' was redubbed

Close up of full color World War II 25th Infantry SSI.

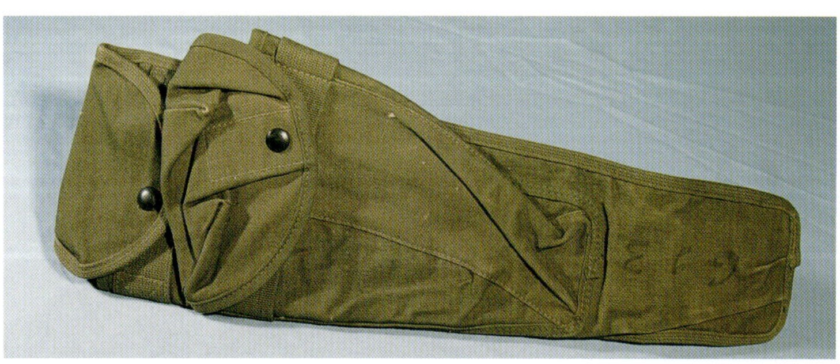

Close up showing the early PRC/10 spare bag. Note the second buttoned pouch that the later model will do away with.

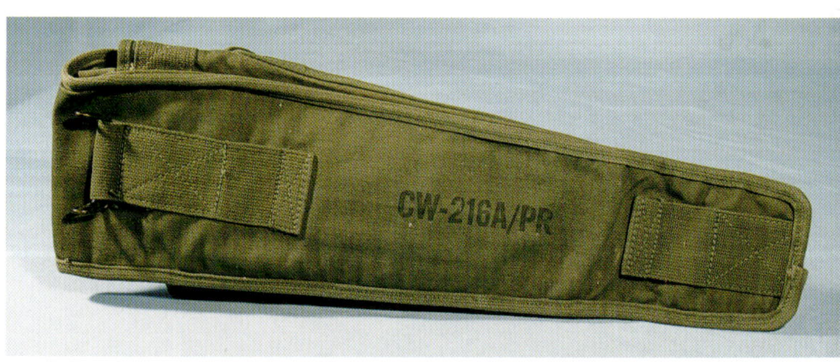

Close up showing the rear of the spare's bag. Note also the M1910 "hook" fastener used instead of the slide keepers of most M1956 items.

Front view of 1st Cavalry Trooper.

Left side.

'WHITE WING' to mollify President Johnson's concern over public opinion. Militarily it would become known as the Bong Son campaign. For forty-two days, the "First Team" hopped across the ridges crowding the South China Sea, the waves of helos depositing Battalions of troops into sandy fortified villages and lush, verdant strongholds. The 1st Cav. soon found themselves up against the 2d VC, and the 18th and 22d NVA Regiments, who fought with determination. Company C of the 2d Battalion, 7th Cavalry, air assaulted Jan. 28 into a hamlet studded landing zone at Phung Du. It was quickly pinned down by a vicious cross fire from a battalion of entrenched V.C."[17]

This Cav. Trooper wears—oddly enough—a Navy/Marine wet weather parka. The parka, which was a pull over garment, features a hood, adjustable cuffs, and two large side "slash" pockets. They were produced in several types, the first being made out of heavy cotton duck, and the newer variation being very similar to the poncho, which were lightweight rubberized material. This model is the early variation. LBE consists of cotton H-suspender connected to a M1956 pistol belt, with two early model M1956 universal pouches. The small grommet in each of the pull-tabs was done away with by 1959. On either side of the universal pouches is a single one-quart canteen and canvas M1956 cover.

"In 1964, a nylon resin-impregnated helmet liner, which gave additional ballistic protection, was introduced to the Army supply system. The internal web suspension and headband were modified, and the neckband was replaced with a newer version that eliminated the need for the leather chinstrap."[18] Attached to the outer camouflage cover are strips of burlap called "scrim." Slung over his shoulder, via a general-purpose (GP) strap, is an

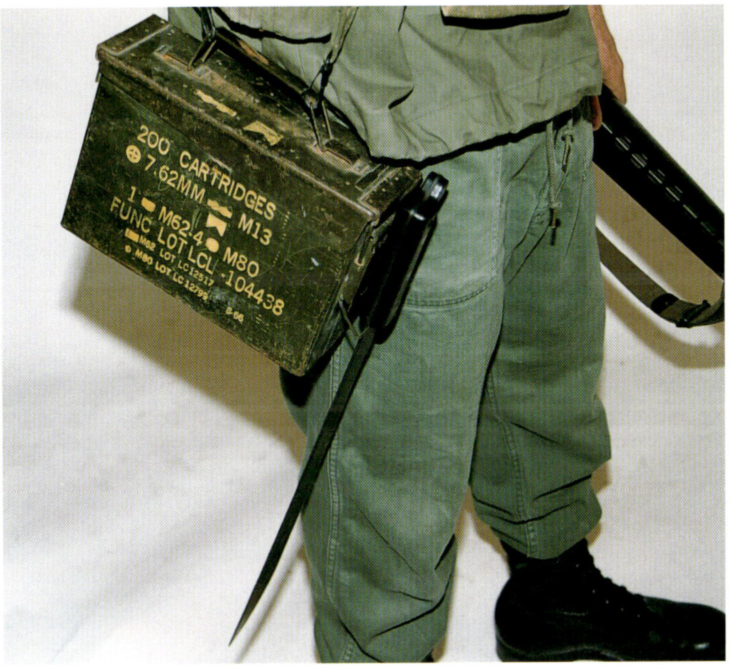

Close up M1942 machete and ammo can.

Close up showing the Navy wet weather parka. Note the draw tabs at the bottom and the metal buttons on the cuffs.

Right side of Cavalry Trooper.

M-60 ammo can with a M1942 machete through the handle. Although the machete was usually issued with the M1944 pattern sheath, this soldier has chosen to improvise and carry it here. MacNamara black combat boots are worn here. Weapon is the early model M16 with the three prong flash suppressor, which came in handy for opening crates of C-rations.

1st Battalion, 27th Infantry "Wolfhounds," 25th Infantry Division, "Operation Fort Smith" Cu Chi, 1966
Rifleman

"The 'Tropic Lightning' 25th Infantry Division was emplaced west of Saigon at the start of the year, and its second Brigade assumed operational responsibilities for the future divisional base camp near Cu Chi. The division's placement directly challenged the prime V.C. lifeline to Cambodian supply points, which was guarded by a maze of V.C. fortifications and tunnel networks. Hau Nghia and Tay Ninh provinces represented a dangerous slice of terrain covered by swamp and jungle, which was never effectively subdued throughout the length of the war."[19]

The armor vest (armor, body), fragmentation, protective, upper torso, M-1952, worn here is especially designed to provide protection against low velocity shells, mortar, and grenade fragments. The vest consists of a ballistic fiber encased in a waterproof envelope of vinyl film inserted into a fabric cover. The fabric cover has two "bellows" patch pockets and flaps, which are closed with a snap fastener. The front of the vest is closed with a zipper and an additional flap covering. The vest also features elastic side laces on either side for fitting, grenade hangers over each front pocket, and shoulder loops. When properly worn, the flak vest will protect vital areas against fragments, which cause most combat casualties. Seen here in one of the grenade hangers, the engineer has placed his white C-rat. Spoon. A green dyed T-shirt was the uniform top for "Operation Fort Smith," while the normal fatigue top was discarded. "Trouser are the second model jungle fatigues which are identical to the first model fatigues, but by 1964-65 the buttons on the pockets were concealed beneath a flap to prevent snagging. The large cargo pockets retained the leg tie downs, and the button take-up tabs along the waist band."[20]

LBE is worn over the flak vest, although it was intended to be worn underneath. He has a cotton H-harness connected to the standard M1956 pistol belt, along with two universal pouches, E-tool and carrier, three canteens, and a butt-pack. Note the diversity in canteens—he carries both the plastic and metal canteens.

In his hand is a captured Chi-Com rifle, found in a tunnel complex near Cu Chi.

'ront view of 25th soldier. Note the white plastic spoon still in the wrapper and ıe red lens on his angle head flashlight.

Full view of the back and LBE of 25th Inf. Soldier.

oldiers wearing the OG 107 cotton sateens and black combat boots unload a hopper from one side while soldiers on the opposite side seem to be loading aptured equipment. Note the bicycle tire underneath the nose of the chopper. J.S. Army Photo.)

Full front view of 25th Infantry Division Soldier.

Full right side of trooper. Note the single plastic 1qt canteen in its M1956 carrier on the small M1956 buttpack.

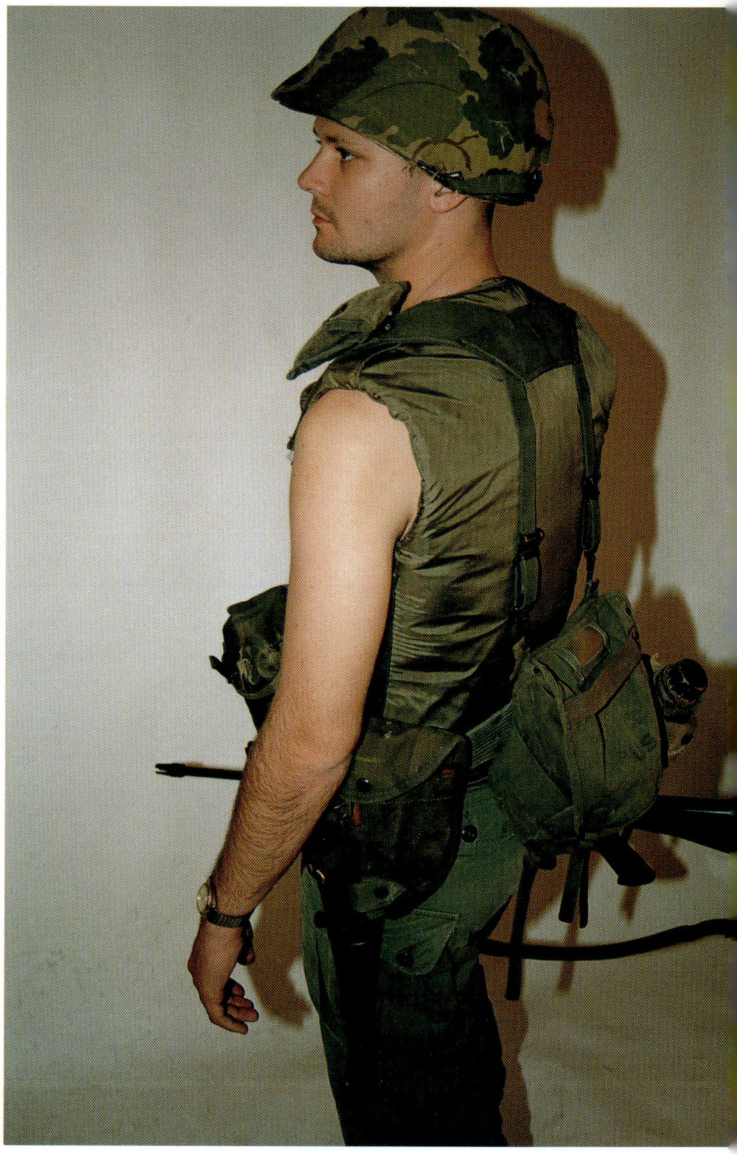

Left side view shows the combination E-tool with the M7 bayonet in its M8A1 scabbard. Also note the lack of a helmet band.

25th soldier kneeling shows off captured Chi-Com rifle.

3

1967

3d Battalion, 60th Infantry "Wild Ones," (Mobile Riverine Force), 9th Infantry Division Operation "Coronado IV," Rung Sat Special Zone, 1967 M-60 Gunner

"There was a significant obstacle to the introduction of U.S. infantry troops into the Mekong Delta. The dense population and agriculture emphasis of the region meant that there was no land available for basing a sizable force. The necessary land would have to be taken, thus providing the VC with invaluable propaganda 'ammunition.' Gen. Westmoreland solved the problem by adopting an idea thought up originally by a U.S. Navy officer, Capt. David F. Welch. In much the same way that U.S. forces in, for example, the Seminole Wars and the Civil War, had used the waterways to facilitate military operations, why could we not create special units equipped to utilize the waterways of the Delta to get at the VC?

So, the Mobile Riverine Force was born; in the planning stages it was dubbed the Mekong Delta Mobile Afloat Force. The Navy part of the force was called the Riverine Assault Force and was

Sgt. Jack Applegate 3/39 Infantry, 9th Div. in the village of Rach kien, March 1967. Note the new Car-15 with the makeshift sling. This weapon is unusual for line troops at this time. On his head he wears a locally produced 2-piece black beret. (Courtesy Jack Applegate)

Photo of two soldiers from an unidentified unit. The Sgt. First class (Right) utilizing the radio wears a second model set of the Jungle fatigues. Note the E-7 chevrons are either the iron type or are drawn on the shirt. Around his neck is a "drive on" rag made of camouflage parachute material. The man on the left appears to be an officer, due to the mustache. He wears an OG 107 cotton sateen uniform shirt, with 1st model "exposed button" trousers. Note the private purchase stag horn handle knife that is secured to his H-harness. (U.S. Army photo)

Two members of the 9th Inf. Div. show captured M-1 carbines and a World War II Russian rifle from a weapons cache in the delta. The man on the left wears a poplin Genuine Trooper private purchase shirt, while the soldier on the right wears a third model poplin shirt with a crude 9th Inf. Div SSI and Spc. 4 rank. Unit unknown.

Sgt. Applegate stands in front of 1st squad, 1st platoons CQ, Rach Kien, wearing 3rd model poplin fatigues with subdued U.S. Army, name strip, C.I.B., E-5 Chevrons, and full color 9th Div. SSI. Note the Vietnamese "cowboy" hat and the small American flag hanging in the upper left corner. The sign reads "AAA-O," 19 July 1967. (Courtesy Jack Applegate)

Sgt. Hunt and Sgt. Applegate in the village of Rach Kien. The 3/39th Infantry occupied half of the village. Both men wear 3d model jungle fatigues and Vietnamese made "cowboy" hats. Sgt. Applegate (left) is enjoying a warm can of Fallstaff beer. (Courtesy Jack Applegate).

given the number designation Task Force 117. It was made up of a large fleet of converted landing crafts supported by several converted LST Hulls that were re-designated as barracks and repair vessels. The small craft were equally divided into river Assault Squadrons; the support vessels constituted their own administrative unit, known as River Support Squadron 7."[21]

"The Mobile Riverine Force (MRF) was made up of River Assault Flotilla One, River Assault Squadron Seven, and the 2d Brigade of the U.S. Army's 9th Infantry Division consisting of the 3d Battalion, 47th Infantry, the 4th Battalion, 47th Infantry, and the 3d Battalion, 60th Infantry. The MRF units began to arrive in Vietnam in January of 1967. After joint in-country training in the Rung Sat Zone the MRF moved out to the Delta and were quartered on 11 ships at the Mobile Riverine Base at Dong Tam, near My To.[22] The base was named by Gen. Westmoreland meaning in Vietnamese "United Hearts and Minds." The new base was unusual in having been created by the Navy Sea Bees and the Army's Corps Of Engineers, who had dredged up sand from the bottom of the My Tho River and made land where there had previously been none. Gen Westmoreland described it as "one of the dustiest places on Earth," but it served its purpose."[23]

The 7.62 M-60 General Purpose Machine Gun was the main platoon automatic weapon for the entire war. The M-60 Machine gun is an air-cooled, belt-fed, gas operated automatic weapon. It fires from the open bolt position, and the ammunition is fed into the gun by a disintegrating metallic split link belt. The gun can

Two members of the 3/39th RECON Platoon in Saigon take time to have their photo taken at one of the many studios. The man on the left wears an ERDL boonie hat that was locally manufactured, along with matching U.S. ERDL poplin camouflage fatigues. The man on the right wears third model OD poplin fatigues with a U.S. made name strip; Brown, with a Vietnamese made U.S. Army and hand sewn C.I.B. On his left sleeve is a twill 9th Infantry SSI. Headgear is a U.S. M1951 style cap. Around his neck is an OD green "drive on" rag. Circa 1967-68. (Madrigal collection.)

Lt. Mandrigal (center) leaves the village of Rach Kien for a night ambush patrol. He wears third model jungle fatigues with pin on LT. rank and crossed rifles, along with twill 9th SSI. Around his waist is a captured Chi-Com SKS ammunition pouch, which was worn very seldom by him due to its worthlessness. The RTO behind him carries the platoon AN/PRC-25 radio and wears no LBE. Around his waist he has secured a cotton bandoleer for extra M-16 twenty round magazines. Note the color pin on C.I.B. The third man also wears no LBE and carries a WP grenade inside its "tootsie roll." All three men wear poplin boonie hats. The two men on the left are RF/PF. (Mandrigal collection)

Full front view of "Mobile Riverine Force" M60 gunner. Note the extra protection his pistol is providing in a very delicate area.

Close up showing the M60 gunner's chow socks and ammo.

fire 100 rounds per minute on Sustained fire, 200 rounds on rapid, and approximately 550 rounds per minute on the Cyclic. Its maximum range is 3,725 meters, while the maximum effective range is 1,100 meters. The "Pig," as it was affectionately known, weighs 23 lbs. unloaded. The M-60 is a crew served weapon and requires a crew of three—two minimum—to effectively operate the gun. The Gunner carries three 100 round bandoleers, with one attached to the gun, while the Asst. Gunner carries three 100 round bandoleers and the ammo bearer, when available, carries the same. Basic load is 600-900, but combat conditions will dictate more.

Uniform worn here is the third and final model in cotton poplin. The fatigue top is worn void of any patches. Although subdued insignia was authorized beginning on 9 June 1966, the change over would take some time, and a mixture of full color and subdued was not uncommon. The lack of any patches shows this is probably a new uniform, and the "pig-man" has not had a chance to go to one of the local tailor shops at Dong Tam to have any insignia put on.

"The 7.62mm ammunition for the M60 is carried in two ways. The cotton bandoleer could be hung from the shoulder, or as here,

Sgt. Applegate next to team hooch. Rach Kien, April, 1967. He wears a 3rd model poplin shirt with no nametape, a subdued U.S. Army strip, and subdued E-5 rank and 9th Div. patch, both being locally made. Headgear is a private purchase ERDL poplin beret with some type of device on the side. Again, he carries his coveted CAR-15. Note the elaborate living conditions in the villages. (Courtesy Jack Applegate.)

St Applegate geared up and ready for action. Uniform is the OG 107's, along with M1 steel pot, 2 bandoleers of 5.56, 100 rounds of M60 ammo, Claymore bag filled with extra mags for his M-16, and four M26 hand grenades complete his fighting load. (Courtesy Jack Applegate.)

Full right side provides a good view of M60 machine gun and two chow socks.

Full figure shot of the M60 gunner, ready to put the gun into action.

Full left side provides for a good view of 9th Infantry patch. Note also the brand new M1956 canteen cover with the nylon trim, which had just come out in late 1967.

Additional full body shot.

Close up showing the two boot socks being utilized to carry the C-rat cans. Note the orange tips on the M60 ammo, these are the "tracers."

Sgt. Applegate kneels in front of living quarters. He wears the third and final pattern of OG 107 cotton sateens with subdued Army and name strip, along with a color C.I.B. On his sleeve is a Color U.S. made SSI 9th Div. and Vietnamese made Sgt. Rank. (Courtesy Jack Applegate) 09 April '67 Rach Kien.

Right: *Company A, 3rd/39th "Chie Hoi" scout, Le Phuoc, stands in company area in front of platoon laundry. He wears 3rd and final model poplin jungle fatigues with a subdued name and U.S. Army strip, along with a full color 9th Div. SSI and a small "beer can" 9th insignia. His scarf is a piece of parachute silk. (Courtesy Jack Applegate)*

Close up of private purchase Army Notebook. This would be used for making "Range cards."

LT. Mandrigal, center w/boonie, is congratulated for outstanding work by 3rd o the 39th Battalion commander LTC. DeLuca in front of Battalion sign ("AAA-O"). Note all three men wear third model poplin jungle fatigues. The LTC has numerous pens and pencils in his pockets and wears an odd nylon coated two magazine pouch usually worn by M.P.s and/or Air Force Personnel. Note the strange tiger stripe pattern of LT. Mandrigal boonie hat and the CAR-15 slung over his shoulder with 30 round magazine. 1967-68. (Mandrigal collection)

Typical in-country made plaque from the 4th Infantry Division in 1967. The plaque is presented to Capt. David J Bungay from the orderly room of A Co. 4th S&T BN. The plaque features a large "Beer can" 4th Div insignia with a map of S. Vietnam and both an American and S. Vietnamese flag.

LT. Mandrigal with Bn. Commander. This is a better shot of his CAR-15 with the 30 round magazine, very unusual for 1967. (Madrigal collection.)

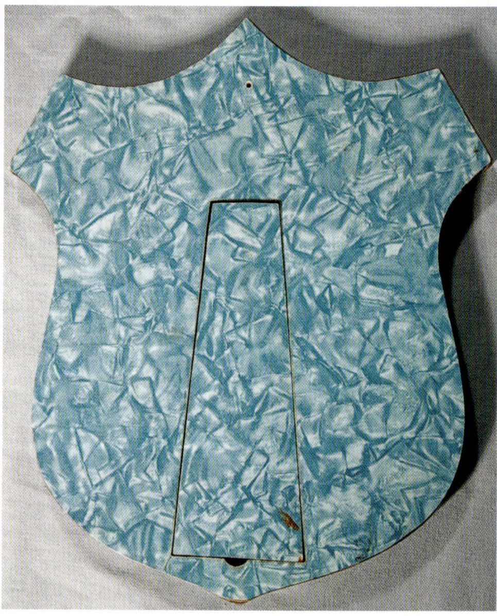

Backside of same plaque.

belts of 150 rounds of disintegrating links are draped around his torso. Note the orange tips on every fifth round, indicating a 'tracer.' The issue OD green towel was often worn around the neck as shown, so that it could be used to wipe the face free of sweat and grime as well as protecting the neck from heavy equipment digging into his shoulders."[24]

Web gear consists of a pistol belt connected to the standard H-harness, along with two universal pouches, which would contain weapons oil, Medium, LSI oil. The universal pouches also contained magazines for his .45 auto pistol, cleaning equipment, bore brush, cleaning swabs, ruptured cartridge extractor, combination wrench, note book and pen for the range card, and a few loose rounds that would be used to remove the stock group. Next to the ammo pouch is an M1956 canteen cover, with plastic canteen. On the rear of the pistol belt, the gunner has secured a heavy nylon coated OD poncho. The two green boot socks, or "chow socks," contain a few day rations. Note the unusual place the gunner has chosen to carry his .45 auto pistol in its black M1916 holster for "extra" protection. "His M17 Chemical-Biological Field Mask in its carrier is correctly worn strapped to his left hip. Anti-riot agents, such as CS, were commonly used to clear VC tunnels, and bunker complexes and U.S. troops used the masks as routine protection."[25] The M1 helmet is worn with the accompanying Helmet Band Camouflage, used here to secure a pack of Pall Malls and a red civilian tooth brush.

Close up showing the M1 helmet with Mitchell pattern cover, and the Vietnamese made C.M.B. pinned to helmet band. Note the bottle of bug juice and the first aid dressing.

4th Battalion, 12th Infantry,
196th Infantry Brigade (Light)
Long Bihn Province, 1967
Medic

Doc, as they were commonly known, wears a first model poplin jungle jacket with no insignia other than a full color, hand sewn shoulder sleeve insignia of the 199th. By this time, most combat units had received the new Tropical combat uniform, or

Full front of 199th Infantry Brigade (Light) Medic. Note he carries an M16 rifle instead of an M1911 pistol.

Good view of the Medic's lightweight ruck with the medical backpack secured to the top of the frame.

Close up of the 199th "Red Catcher" SSI. Note the great detail the Vietnamese tailor went through while hand sewing this patch.

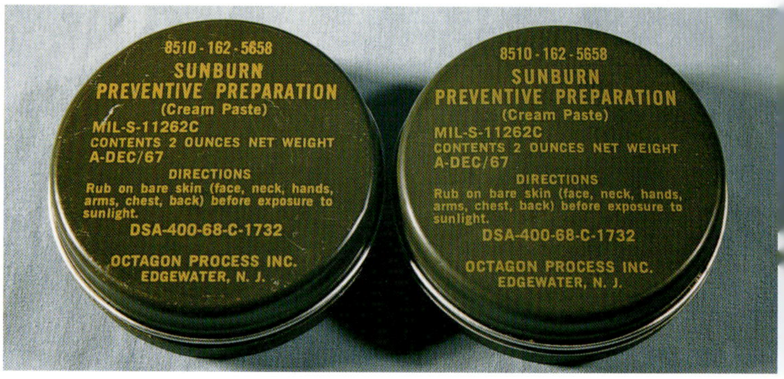

Close up showing two cans of the Sunburn Preventive Preparation; cream paste. Both are dated Dec/'67.

"Jungle Fatigues," as they would be known. The trousers he wears are the third model, lacking the tie-down straps in the thigh pockets and the buttoned tightening tabs on the waistline. Around his neck, the medic has chosen an OD green towel for protection from the hot sun.

LBE consists of a M1956 pistol belt without the cotton H-harness for support, two universal pouches on his left side, and a single M26 "lemon" grenade. On his right side, he has two of the newer 1967 cotton canteen covers, which feature a nylon trim

Close up of upper torso of medic provides a good view of the "exposed buttons" of his jungle fatigue shirt and the straps to his Lightweight rucksack.

LTC Myron E. Lee, Commander; "SPIKER 6" 2nd Battalion, 39th Infantry, 9th I.D. (Courtesy A.J. Allen)

Capt. John R. Knightly, Battalion S-3. Note his 1st model exposed buttons with full color BOS and U.S. Army strip. On his left sleeve he wears a RANGER tab. (Courtesy A.J. Allen)

Headquarter sign in front of Company area. (Courtesy A.J. Allen)

Company A officers, XO LT Hopkins, LT Kuts-Cheraux, LT Greer, LT Valle, and LT Maniccia. All Lieutenants wear the 3d model poplins except LT. Maniccia, who wears the second model OG 107 sateens. Note the different style hats. (Courtesy A.J. Allen)

V.C. weapons captured by the 2nd of the 39th on OPERATION AKRON II. (Courtesy A.J. Allen.)

Two full color 9th Infantry Division SSI. Both are WWII surplus and are different sizes.

C Company officers (left to right) LT Madden, LT Peck, LT Kiser, and 2nd LT Hoppe. The two on the right wear the 3d model jungle fatigues with subdued 9th div.'s, while the two on the left wear second model OG 107 sateens. (Courtesy A.J. Allen.)

Co. E LT Gillespie, Capt. Given, LT Stanley, and LT. Grabher. Note that LT Gillespie wears "airborne" wings on his shirt and his baseball cap. (Courtesy A.J. Allen)

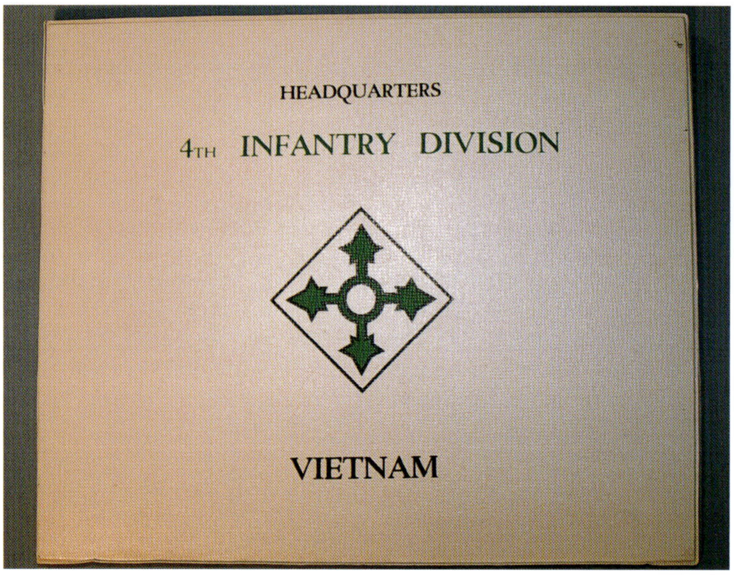

Close up showing a Vietnamese made binder for awards such as a Bronze Star. These could hold and display two official award presentations.

Rifleman from the 173rd (Airborne) 1-503rd, Dak To, prepares all his ammunition, grenades, and Claymore mine for easy access. Along with the two cotton M16 bandoleers on the berm, he wears an additional one across his chest. Note the hastily prepared defensive trench.

along the top (not to be confused with the M1967 gear, which is all nylon). Around his waist is the canvas M17 carrier for the M17 protective mask. Worn across his chest is a cotton bandoleer with only four 20 round magazines in it. Connected to the upper half of his Lightweight rucksack frame is the medical field pack, which could hold the larger bandages, an instrument set, Gelusil, Vaseline gauze, field medical cards, and saline ringers, along with numerous cough drops and aspirin and other assorted medical items in its many pockets. It also featured a rectangular pocket on the side for a wooden splint.

"His steel pot is fitted with the 'Mitchell' pattern helmet cover and the issue green elastic Camouflage, Helmet, Band which was initially intended as a camouflage aid, but was more typically used in Vietnam to hold small items. Here, the medic has secured an additional bandage and a bottle of bug juice."[26] Pinned to the front is a gold Vietnamese sand-cast Combat Medical Badge (C.M.B.). The Medic also carries an M-16A1 rifle.

4th Battalion, 503rd Infantry,
173rd (Airborne) Brigade
Hill 875, November 1967
Grenadier

"The opening rounds of the battle of Dak To actually started in June 1967 when mortars pounded the U.S. Army Special Forces camp at Dak To, situated in the mountains of central Kontum Province. The monsoon season blanketed the region with low clouds and moving ground fog, but two paratrooper battalions of the 173d Airborne Brigade managed to airlift into Dak To on June 17th. The operation would be initially tagged GREELEY. It would span a rugged wilderness covered by thick double and triple canopy jungle. On June 22, a company of the 2nd Battalion, 503 Infantry (Airborne), clashed with the 6th Battalion, 24th NVA Regiment in one of the most violent battles of the Vietnam war. That morning, Company A left its night position in the triple canopy jungle and began heading toward the brigade command post at Dak To. By late afternoon, the point squad collided with a

Full front and left of the paratrooper Grenadier, Dak To 1967.

Full right side of 173d "Sky Soldier" shows his 45 pistol in the black holster.

Upper torso giving emphasis on his left side. Note the two piece 173d patch subdued, along with his 2nd model 2qt canteen and cover.

North Vietnamese Army force, and the battle quickly engulfed the 'Sky-Soldiers.' Artillery fire and helicopter delivered rockets pierced the dark green foliage. All failed to check the assault. By 11:00 A.M., all contact was lost, until a small band of survivors stumbled into the Company lines. Companies B and C were ordered forward at once. Company C was able to reach the area by 14:00 hours, but heavy ground fire repulsed them and they were not able get to the area of the lost men. Early the next day, the paratroopers were able to sweep the area where the platoons had made their last stand. There they found the crumpled bodies of seventy-six dead paratroopers. For the next few months, members of the 3d Brigade of the 1st Cavalry division, the Vietnamese 5th and 8th ARVN Airborne, a Batt. of the 42d, ARVN Regiment, along with members of the 4th Infantry Division fought against a firmly entrenched NVA in the western Kontum Province. The paratroopers suffered mounting losses in futile attacks on these fortifications."[27]

This Grenadier, from the 4th Bn., 503 INF wears the 3rd model jungle fatigues with all subdued insignia. On his left sleeve is a two piece SSI of the 173rd—one-piece patches are extremely rare and much sought after by collectors.

Worn around his chest is a claymore mine bag filled with thirty 40mm M-79 rounds. During the fierce hill fighting in Nov. Paratroopers carried claymore mine bags filled to the brim with extra magazines and grenades and strapped double over their chest. "As they charged the summit against the well-entrenched NVA, they could easily reach ammunition and rapidly exchange empties for full ones."[28] Additional rounds are carried in a 1-quart canteen cover. Due to the limited number of grenade vests available, many grenadiers like this one had to improvise, adapt, and overcome. Rounds for the weapon were usually carried in the unsatisfactory method of the cotton ammunition bandoleers. "Each bandoleer could accommodate six 40mm rounds, secured in 2 three round plastic egg crate. The cotton bandoleers were flimsy, ripped easily, and wore through rapidly, and could not accommodate the grenadier with enough rounds for his basic fighting load, which was 27 rounds, which meant the soldier would have to carry 5 bandoleers. Grenadiers complained that carrying several bandoleers also created uncomfortable weight imbalances and hindered easy one handed access to the rounds in their bandoleer pockets."[29] Some soldiers remedied this by utilizing empty claymore bags to hold the 40mm rounds; two bags could double their

Close up showing the AN/PRR-9 receiver connected to the back of his M1 helmet.

Close up showing date on Spike Protective Jungle boots. June 1967; 11N 67.

fighting load. At this time, the grenadier carried an additional weapon, an M1911, .45 cal. Pistol. In years to come, many would carry an additional rifle, an M-16, before the adoption of the over/under combo XM148.

Web gear is made up of a M1956 belt, along with an H-harness, one universal pouch, a 1-quart canteen and cover, a black leather holster for his .45 cal M1911 pistol, and an early 2nd model prototype 2-quart collapsible canteen/with carrier. "The M-17 Field Protective Mask in its carrier is worn in the leg-carry position, with the shoulder strap used as a waist strap, and the waist strap used as a leg strap."[30] These masks were invaluable due to the use of CS-RIOT agents to clear the numerous NVA out of bunkers and tunnel complexes that circled the hill. Connected to his M-1 steel pot is the new AN/PRR-9 Helmet Mounted Radio Receiver, along with the AN/PRT-4 Hand Held Transmitter, which is seen here secured to the left side of his H-harness. The new "walkie-talkie" type system was designed to provide communication between the members of a rifle platoon, but due to a number of shortcomings, the sets were used in LP/OPs and static defense. The system worked well only if you could see the person you were trying to communicate with.

Full figure view of II Field Force LRRP, 1967.

Black & White photo of LRRP.

Company F, 51st Infantry, (Airborne) LRPs,
II Field Force, Vietnam
Long Bihn, 1967
LRPs

"On 25 September 1967 the II Field Force Vietnam gained its own ground reconnaissance when Co. F, 51st Infantry (airborne) was activated. The Companie's mission, upon completion of training, was providing long-range reconnaissance and Intel appraisal directly to the operations staff at field level. Company F was formed from experienced personnel and equipment acquired from the 173rd Airborne Brigade LRRP platoon. Recon personnel of the Co. were known as the 'Hurricane Patrollers' after the signal code word 'hurricane.' Starting on 8 Oct 1967, each patrol member was sent through reconnaissance training at the MACV Recondo school in Nha Trang. The course ensured a solid foundation of RECONDO qualified personnel. After the members completed schooling, they were sent back to Company F at Long Binh. The Co. was then placed under the helicopter equipped 'Red Horse' 3d Squadron, 17th Cav. for aerial support and conducted exercises in hostile areas of Gia Dinh Province. The consolidated unit provided II Field Force with a highly flexible air-ground reconnaissance battalion. The force provided support to the 199th Inf. Brigade and 101st Airborne Div through January. Teams var-

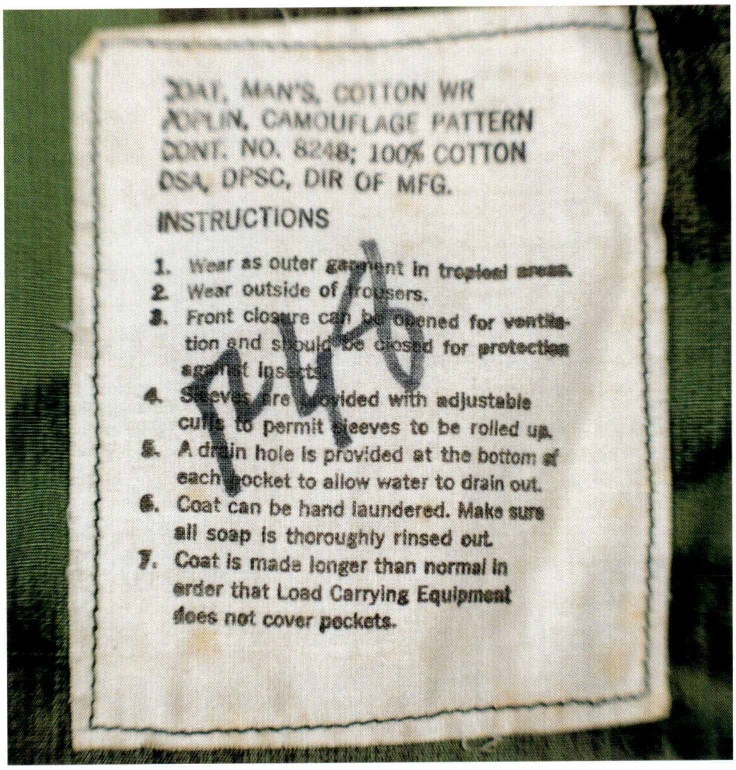

Close up showing the tag for the ERDL Poplin; Coat, Man's Cotton WR Poplin, Camouflage Pattern, with no date. The WR stands for Wind Resistant. Circa 1967.

Full figure shot of LRRP in B&W.

Example of a typical ERDL "Poplin" shirt.

Close up of July 1967 edition of the Ranger handbook.

Close up of two different variations of Spc. 5 rank. The full color one on the left is U.S. produced while the subdued one on the right is a Vietnamese handmade variation.

ied in size, and were changed from 6 man teams to 5 man teams in 1968."[31]

The ERDL camo tropical uniform is shown here in its short lived cotton poplin version. The uniform was styled identically to the third pattern tropical combat uniform and included the same design features. "Camouflage clothing was introduced to the army during WWII, and post war studies of the spectral characteristics of commercial dyes made it possible to formulate both visual and infrared camouflage. The ERDL was technically restricted, being distributed first to pathfinders and reconnaissance combat units during 1968."[32] "That same year, Co F 51st INF stated that the poplin material was too thin and ripped easily when wet. The LRRPs also stated that the uniform could not withstand Vietnam's thick vegetation in which the long-range Patrols operated."[33] On the left sleeve of his shirt is a U.S. twill 2nd Field Force patch, along with a Vietnamese manufactured AIRBORNE ARC. On both sleeves he wears locally made E-6 Chevrons.

LBE consists of mostly M1956 gear, to include two universal pouches, web belt, two canteens with covers, and the cotton H suspenders. Taped to the suspenders are both the AN/PRT 4 transmitter and the helmet mounted AN/PRR-9 receiver for inner squad communication. These worked well only if you could see the person you were trying to talk with. The locally produced tigerstripe beret, seen here, was used in the Vietnamese Marine Corps. "Sea Wave" Pattern has been personalized by the addition of a hand woven LRRP arc above a subdued parachute badge. Around his neck is the triangular bandage worn "cowboy" style. Weapon is the M-16A1 with green duct tape on the hand-guard and stock to help break up the outline.

Close up showing two bottles of the clear bug juice. Both are dated 4/66, but note the different caps on the two.

Close up of two packs of C-rat cigarettes.

Front view of Asst. gunner from the 196th Infantry Brigade.

Left side view showing the full color 196th "Burning Rope" patch.

2d Battalion, 1st Infantry (Light Infantry), 196th (Light) Infantry Brigade Chu Lai, 1967 Assistant. Gunner

"The 196th Infantry Brigade was raised at Fort Devens and was originally scheduled to be sent to the Dominican Republic in mid-1966, but was rushed to Vietnam instead and posted in the western portion of the III Corps Tactical Zone. It initiated the operation into War Zone C, of Tay Ninh Province, which developed into a major action after a large enemy base camp was uncovered 19 October 1966. In April 1967 the Brigade was selected, along with the 1st Brigade 101st Airborne Division and the 3d Brigade, 25th Infantry Division, to form a provisional division sized unit called Task Force OREGON, and then moved to the I corps Tactical Zone. The Brigade stayed with this command, which was converted into the 23d Infantry Division (Americal) 25 September 1967. The 196th Infantry Brigade officially joined this Division 15 February 1969."[34] "The 2nd Battalion, 1st Infantry was part of the 196th Infantry Brigade and was one of the last Infantry Battalions to depart Vietnam."[35]

Tropical combat uniform worn here is the third and final version produced in the cotton poplin material. Subdued insignia was authorized for all field and work uniforms in late 1966, but the changeover period would take a while, and it was not uncommon to see a mixture of full-color and subdued insignia together. On the left sleeve is the 196th SSI. Worn over the shoulder of the

Right/back side showing the spare barrel bag.

Provides a full shot of the back and the bag.

Close up of spare barrel bag and the bandoleer of M60 ammo. Note the M1966 pistol belt.

Close up of Asst. gunners 3d and final model poplin trousers. Note the take up tabs have been replaced with the take up "draw-tabs." These are still in use on U.S. fatigues today.

Close up of 3d model trouser tags and button fly.

Close up of large tag inside 3d and final model poplin shirt worn by the Asst. Gunner. Note the date, 1967 as evident by the DSA-100-67-C-0146.

Close up of small tag inside 3d-model poplin shirt.

Close up with emphasis on the left side showing the 196th patch and the two waxy boxes for his ammo.

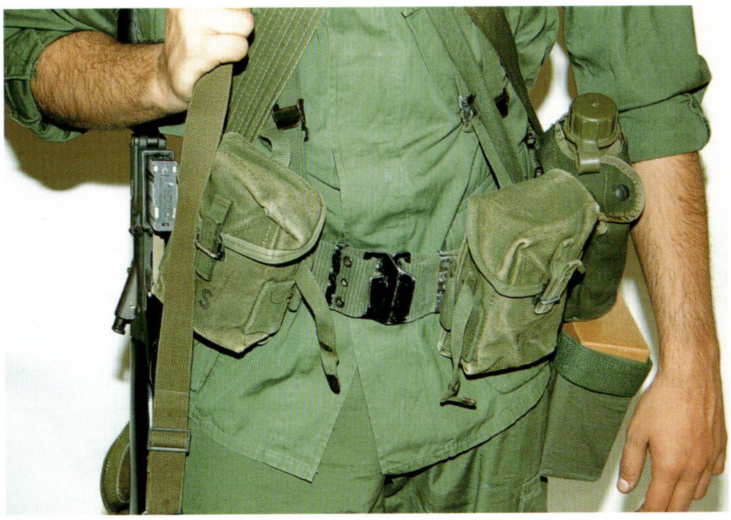

Close-up showing universal pouches and Davis fastener on his M1966 (D) pistol belt. Note the nylon trim on the canteen cover.

Close up showing the private purchase notebook (right) and the GI one on the (left).

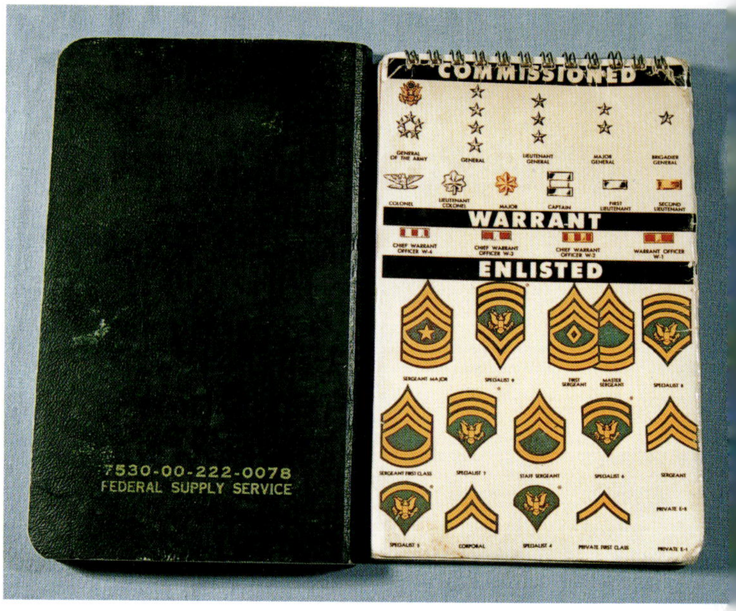

Close up of the backs of the two notebooks. The inside flap of the civilian mode has more information like rank structure, and lines for the CO's name and such

Asst. gunner is the rubber coated spare barrel case. This contained the spare barrel, asbestos mittens for changing the hot barrel, cleaning rod, combination wrench, ruptured cartridge extractor, and a bore, chamber, and receiver brush. Along with the case, the Asst. gunner also carried the T&E, or traversing and elevating mechanism. "Ammunition is packaged in 2 waxy cardboard boxes with cotton bandoleers of 100 rounds each, and weighs approximatel seven pounds per 100 rounds."

Web gear consists of two universal pouches, a new M195 canteen cover, and M1966 pistol belt, which features the horizontal weave and the Davis quick release fastener. Weapon is the M16A1.

4

1968

th Battalion,47th Infantry (Riverine Infantry),
th Infantry Division "Mobile Riverine Force"
Iy Tho/Dong Tam, 1968
Recon Platoon Leader

Worn by this Officer is the third and final version of the pop-in jungle fatigues. On his left, he wears a crude twill SSI of the th Inf. Div. Both of his crossed rifles (BOS) and his rank, First .t. Bar, are directly embroidered to his collar tabs, a practice not uncommon for most officers and some NCOs. Both his U.S. Army and C.I.B. are Vietnamese made and probably came from the same local tailor shop, were they could be purchased for about $.25 each. On his left pocket is a circular 4th Battalion, 47th Infantry pocket patch. It features a subdued black Spear- head in the center on top of the Infantry crossed rifles. The patch stood for the Mobile Riverine Force "Spear-headers," of which the 4th, 47th Infantry was a part of. Different variations of this were available

ull figure shot of 4th Bn., 47th Infantry Recon Platoon Leader.

Left side view, providing a good look at the 9th Inf. Div. SSI twill patch and the magazines in his pocket.

Rear shot showing the poncho and two canteens.

Upper torso shot without the gear. Note the 47th Infantry D.I. pin on his pocket flap. This is a good shot of his "Sea Wave" tigerstripe pattern beret.

in color, along with their sister unit, the 3rd Battalion, 47th, and the 3rd Battalion, 60th Infantry, which both had elaborate, colorful pocket patches.

This officer has elected to carry a WWII vintage M-3 "Grease" gun, along with his M1911 colt pistol. Ammunition for the grease gun would not be a problem, since it fired the same pistol round as the .45 cal M1911; the long magazines would be somewhat difficult to obtain, and carry, so this Lt. has chosen to keep them in his cargo pocket of his trousers. Web gear consists of a horizontal weave belt with the ball type fastener. On it, he has at-

Close up showing direct embroidered Crossed rifles (BOS) Infantry, along with his hand stitched U.S. Army strip and Vietnamese made C.I.B.

Close up showing Vietnamese made "MOBILE RIVERINE FORCE 'SPEAR-HEADERS.'" Full color variations were made in light blue, the spear was yellow along with yellow 4 and 47. There is also a 68mm metal pocket badge variation.

lose up of twill SSI 9th Inf. Division.

Close up 9th infantry Division sniper patch being worn on the left pocket of a rip-stop jacket.

lose up 9th Infantry Division Sniper patch, usually worn on left pocket, seen ere on a gold tigerstripe shirt.

*lose up of P*S the Preventative Maintenance Monthly, which is still in use oday and made famous a very sexy character named "sweet 16."*

Members of the 4th of the 47th Infantry, 9th Infantry Division, prepare to move out on the Tango boats, which were WWII landing crafts, seen here in the background. The man with his back to the camera has fashioned a small pack out of a small bag and has tied it to the yoke of his H-harness. On his pistol belt he wears a poncho, which seems to be put on hap-hazardly and secured with a single rubber band. Next to that are two 1-quart canteens, connected to the web belt by a D-ring. The man on the right wears standard issue OG 107s with corporal rank and a Vietnamese produced ammo vest. Note the leggings that keep his trouser tight all the way up to his cargo pocket. The two men in the ERDL fatigues are a sniper team, note the M-14 rifle and the AN/PVS-2 scope over his shoulder, along with what appears to be a poncho. Many times these teams would accompany patrols, usually attached to the HQ element, and had colorful call signs such as "The Gunfighters," "Wyatt Earp," or "Doc Holiday."

U.S. Army photo-9th Div. Note that this soldier wears no rank, but is most likely an NCO or an Officer, evident by the CAR-15 rifle he carries. Also, note the Chi Com. SKS ammunition pouches that he wears to hold his 20 round magazines. Dated 1968. (photographer Kovacs.)

Numerous members of the 9th Inf. Div familiarize themselves with a captured AK-47 in the rain 1968. Note the crude 9th Infantry Div. patches worn.

tached one universal pouch, with additional .45 ammo to be loaded later, due to the lack of available M-3 magazines. On the opposite side he has a single compass/first aid pouch, and on the rear of the pistol belt he has attached an older rubberized poncho, which is folded and tied with 550 para cord. Next to that are two 1-quart canteens with D-rings that are connected to his H-harness. On the front of his harness are a single M18 smoke grenade and an additional D-ring with the "Swiss seat," or 6-foot rope, coiled. This was common with the 9th Inf. Div. due to the inundated delta area in which they operated. Around his neck is a scarf, more commonly known as a "drive on rag," used to wipe the sweat from his face. Headgear is a tigerstripe beret in the Vietnamese Marine Corps, "Sea Wave" pattern, which he wears with no insignia in lieu of a helmet.

Three members of the 9th Inf. Div. parallel a canal sweeping for mines along the banks 19 Feb 1968. Only one man wears the 1969-flak vest and a full color 9th Div patch.

9th Inf. Div. 1968. A platoon medic and other soldiers of the 47th Infantry, 9th Division, fish a dead soldier out of the canal. The medic carries his medical kit bag and carries extra dry socks, along with numerous C-rat toilet papers in his helmet band. Note the man at far right wears a boonie hat and has no helmet.

Recon soldier of the 2d battalion, 47th Infantry, 9th Infantry Division fires his M79 through a window at a VC position during "Mini-Tet" offensive in Saigon, May 11, 1968. In this action, two local force VC Battalions attacked the Y-bridge over the Kinh Doi Canal, which separates downtown Saigon from the urban Nha Be District near the Y-Bridge.

Full shot of the 60 gunner from the 3d of the 7th Infantry gets ready for the assault on the race track.

Company A, 3d Battalion, 7th Infantry,
199th Infantry Brigade (Light)
January 31st, Saigon, Phu Tho Racetrack (Tet), 1968
M60 Gunner

"The 1968 TET offensive began on 31 Jan. 1968 with a 3:00 A.M. rocket attack against the II Field Force Vietnam H.Q. at Long Bihn Post and Bien Hoa Air Base. The 199th Brigade was soon defending itself in fierce combat against the 275th Viet Cong Regiment smashing against them and II Field Force, Vietnam's perimeter. During the attacks, the Brigades 3d Battalion, 7th Infantry was helicoptered into Saigon to retake the Phu Tho Racetrack from the 6th VC LF Battalion, who had infiltrated the capital and were using the racetrack as a command post."[36] "The hub of several main roads, it was a good rallying point for Viet Cong unfamiliar with the city, and its use as a helicopter landing zone was denied to the Americans. Company A, 3d Battalion, 7th Infantry was dispatched to regain the race track. At eight o'clock on the morning of January 31st, 8 armored personnel carries from the brigade's reconnaissance troop and several trucks moved the soldiers downtown toward the objective. Six blocks from the track, heavy automatic weapon fire opened up from rooftops and houses lining the boulevard. The column continued forward for another two blocks as the VC fire intensified. An RPG fired rocket slammed into the lead tracked command carrier, killing three and leaving others dazed and wounded. Dismounted infantry fought from building to building. Recoilless rifle fire blasted holes through walls, and the men tried to fire back as hundreds of panic stricken civilians fled past as the battle raged on. By one o'clock the company had only advanced two more blocks in a series of vicious house to house fighting. The track was taken after eight hours, and for the next two days, the battalion engaged in house to house fighting in the Cholon sector of Saigon."[37]

This 60 gunner wears a 3rd model poplin jungle jacket devoid of any type of subdued U.S. patches. "Tropical combat clothing was developed to sustain a certain degree of comfort for soldiers operating in regions of extreme humidity and heat. Military comfort meant that soldiers were clothed so as to maintain a high rate of activity for several hours before suffering heat exhaustion. The goal was not comfort in the ordinary sense, but the avoidance of acute discomfort that impaired combat efficiency, created critical physiological heat stress, and limited performance."[38] "The 7.62 ammo for his M60 machine gun is draped around his torso and his waist. Though exposing it to dirt and corrosion, this was the common way to carry machine gun ammunition. A 50 round belt is loaded into the feed tray cover and hangs down along the side of the gun."[39] His personal side arm, a .45 pistol, is kept,

Rear view of 60 gunner with hastily prepared lightweight rucksack.

With the assault over, and the race track secured, this 60 gunner prepares to move to another location. Carrying the "Pig" this way is about the only "comfortable" way there is to carry the weapon!

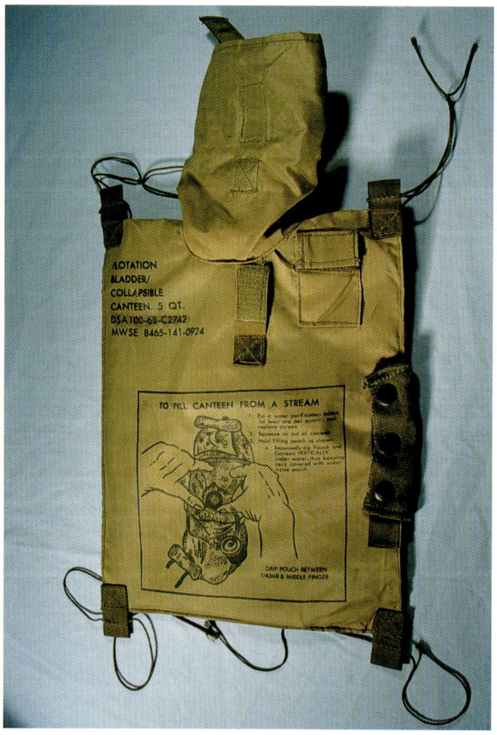

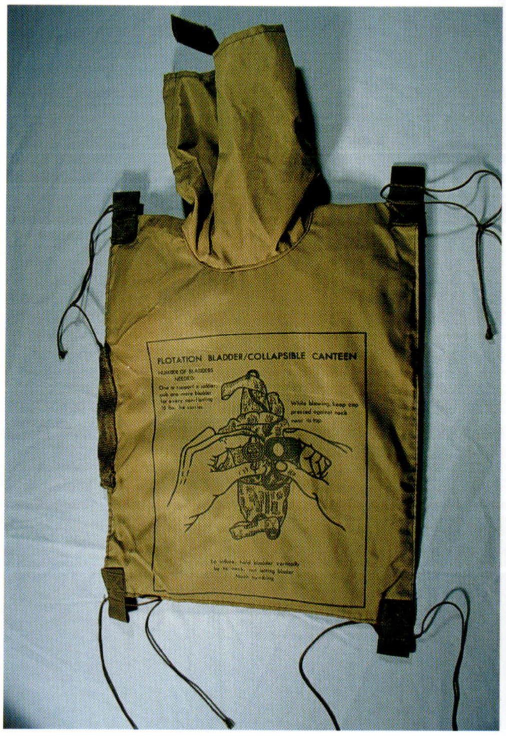

Close up (Left) of the Flotation Bladder/Collapsible Canteen, 5 QT. Note the instruction label printed on it. Close up (Right) of the back of 5QT canteen.

oddly enough, in his pocket, either due to personal choice or the lack of enough M1916 holsters. He wears full M1956 LBE web equipment to include one universal pouch, two 1-quart canteens with covers, and a M1966 vertical weave pistol belt connected to his H-harness. Additional items are carried in his Lightweight rucksack, which is worn high on its Aluminum tubular frame, along with his sleeping gear, a rolled poncho and liner secured hastily above the bag. Attached to the outside of his rucksack are two 1-quart canteens, one in its cover, the other placed inside the M1956 E tool cover, along with a single OD green boot sock full of C-rations. In his double set of M-1 helmet bands he has secured a bottle of insect repellent, "bug-juice," and a bottle of LSA oil for his gun. Around his neck is an OD green towel.

LRRP kneels for a second along the trail, waiting for the hand signal to "move out."

Company F, 58th Infantry (LRP) Team-13,
"Howling Commandos,"
101st (Airborne) Division
Nui Ke Mountains, 1968
Scout

This LRRP, a member of a six-man team, is the teams' leader, or senior scout. Uniform consists of a set of heavy weight tigerstripe camouflage in the "silver" pattern. The shirt features two breast pockets, each with a billow on the inside, and is secured with a single plastic button. Trousers feature two rear, two cargo, and a single "cigarette" pocket on the left leg, initially intended for a first aid dressing packet, which is sealed and contains a sterilized cotton gauze used for emergency dressing of wounds when medical services are not quickly available. Just above it in the cargo pocket are the LRP's notebook, pencil, and map, all in a plastic bag. The right pocket contains a single pop flare. Rucksack is a khaki tan Indigenous pack, which is based on a NVA 3 pocket pack, and is constructed of heavy canvas. Each

Full view of LRRP, note the tan indigenous rucksack and the overall "silver" color of his tigerstripe uniform.

Full view of LRRP.

Full left side of 101st LRRP. Note the single "recon" finger-less glove on his left hand.

Left leg with map and notebook inside, along with small "cigarette" pocket.

of its three outer pockets are capable of holding a single 1qt plastic canteen or other items of that size. Inside he carries his individual first aid kit, a poncho, half of a poncho liner, OD green towel, an AN/PRC battery, 2 cotton bandoleers with a total of 14 twenty round magazines, weapon cleaning kit, signal mirror, and enough rations for the duration of the mission. According to Gary Linderer, Author and LRRP Veteran, most 101st LRRPs carried only "one meal a day." These would consist of the new LRRP dehydrated rations, which were much lighter than the C-rats. Fastened to the right side of his cotton H-harness is a black cardboard container, or "Tootsie roll,"[RT] which houses his morphine suretts, codeine tablets, Dapsone and Tetracycline tablets, along with Blood expander. "Teams were also given new experimental items and classified equipment to test out starting in early 1966,

Close up showing M16A1 rifle with OD green tape. Note, he only wears one "Recon" glove.

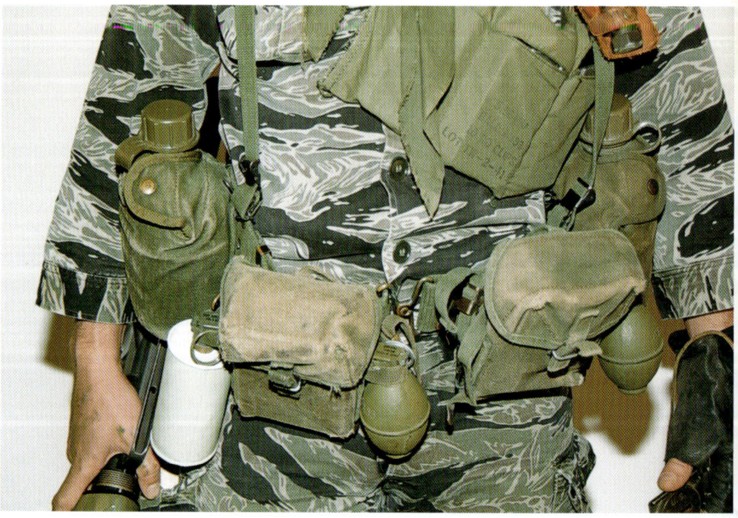

Close up of LBE.

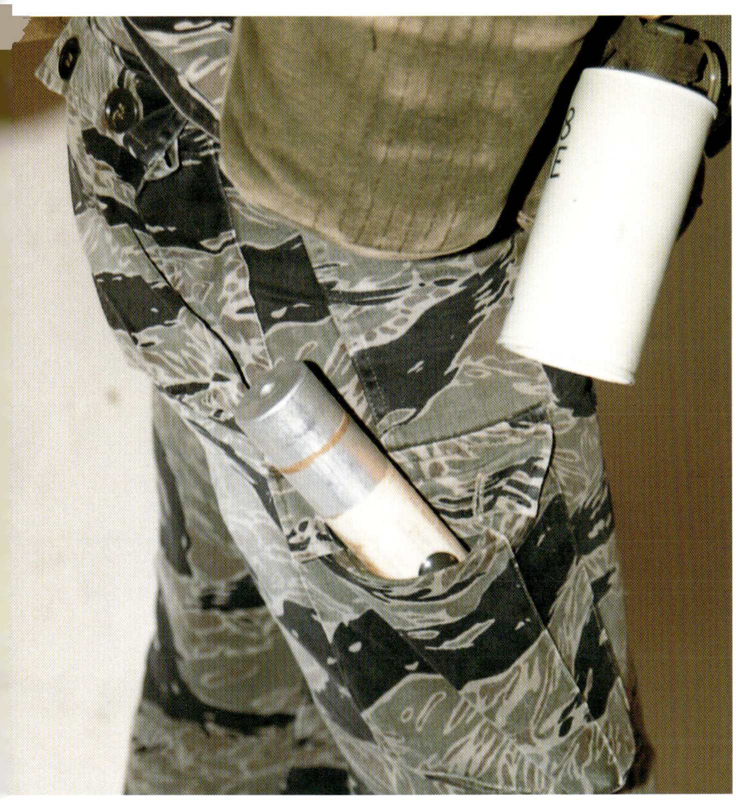

Pop flare.

Close up of right side and "Tootsie roll," which is used to store the M18 smoke grenade. These are used to keep breakable items safe from harm during movement and fire fights.

Close up of left side with Air Force survival knife and plastic container for matches.

such as the new AN/PVS-2 'Starlight' scope and chemical man pack personnel detectors, called "people-sniffers."[40] Taped to the left side is the Air Force survival knife, along with a Waterproof matchbox. The small plastic waterproof matchbox is a means for keeping matches dry and for starting fires by spark ignition in an emergency. The box is a small cylinder shaped, plastic container with a screw cap, a striking disk, and a striking bar. A sealing gasket fits inside the screw cap and provides a tight seal when the cap is screwed onto the cylinder. The striking disk, which is

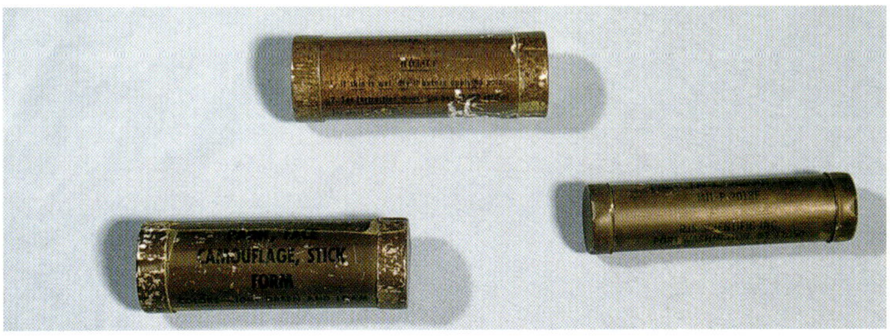

Close up of the Paint, Face, Camouflage Stick, Form, or "Camo" sticks. The top one is dated 1967, bottom left, dated 1968. Both are the size of a roll of quarters. The one at bottom right is dated 1987, and is the size of a roll of dimes. This size is POST war.

Lt. Mandrigal and Recon Platoon Sgt. stand in doorway of 3/39 Recon C.P. Both men wear the poplin ERDL camouflage uniforms. The platoon Sgt. Wears a black Vietnamese made beret with a 75th Infantry DI crest on it, very unusual for 1968. In his "shorty" CAR-15 are three 20 round magazines taped together. Lt. Mandrigal wears a locally produced tiger boonie in a very unique "French style," and holds his CAR-15 with a 30 round magazine. Very unusual for 1968. (Courtesy Madrigal)

Recon platoon members all geared up ready for night ambush. All members wear the new poplin ERDL thanks to Lt. Madrigal trading a captured AK-47 for camouflage uniforms to some REMF in Saigon. Note the man on the far left wears the new grenade vest. The "cowboy" on the far right in sunglasses is their Vietnamese advisor/scout.

mounted on the inside top surface of the cap, has an abrasiv surface for striking safety matches. The striking bar, located o the bottom of the container, is made of a material that produces spark when it is struck with the sharp edge of a knife or som other piece of metal. Connected to his horizontal weave pistc belt are two M1956 "universal" pouches with two M26 grenades and a single M18 smoke. Across his chest is a cotton bandolee with an additional seven 20 round magazines. Headgear is a locally procured boonie hat in the tigerstripe pattern.

His M16A1 rifle has been camouflaged with OD green tape which could be removed and used for securing prisoners, securing bandages to wounds, or repairing tears in his uniform. Aroun his neck is worn the OD green drive on rag.

2nd Battalion, 2nd Infantry (Mechanized),
1st Infantry Division
Quan Loi, 1968
Grenadier

Worn on the front of his M-1 steel pot are the Army's sun wind, and dust goggles, which were mainly used by aircraft mechanics and armored vehicle crewman like this one. Soldiers regularly used them to protect their eyes against dust, dirt, and flying debris thrown up by other vehicles while traveling along any o Vietnam's "Super Highway" dirt roads. The goggles had a clea plastic lens that was intended to be close fitting and featured ar elastic headband that could be adjusted; one size fits all.

Uniform consists of the new "rip-stop" cotton poplin with matching name and U.S. Army strips, both sewn on "rip-stop"

Grenadier from the "Big Red One."

ull figure of Grenadier. Note the contrast in color between his shirt and trousers.

Good view of his left side, showing a full color 1st INF.SSI, along with a U.S. made Spc. 5 rank insignia.

otton poplin material, a hand sewn C.I.B., a twill 4th Infantry SSI on his combat side, SPC 5 rank, and a full color 1st Infantry Division on his service side.

Most Mechanized Infantry Types, like this one, wear minimal web gear. Attached to the front are two of the M1956 Canvas Universal Small Arms Ammunition Cases, that were capable of holding three M16 magazines, with grenade slots on the side, and were constructed of heavy OG 107 cotton duck material. Note the compass/first aid pouch attached to the universal pouch via the grenade slot. Worn on his right side is a single M1956 canteen cover with 1qt canteen. Connected to the rear of his pistol belt is the 2qt collapsible canteen with the water repellent nylon duck

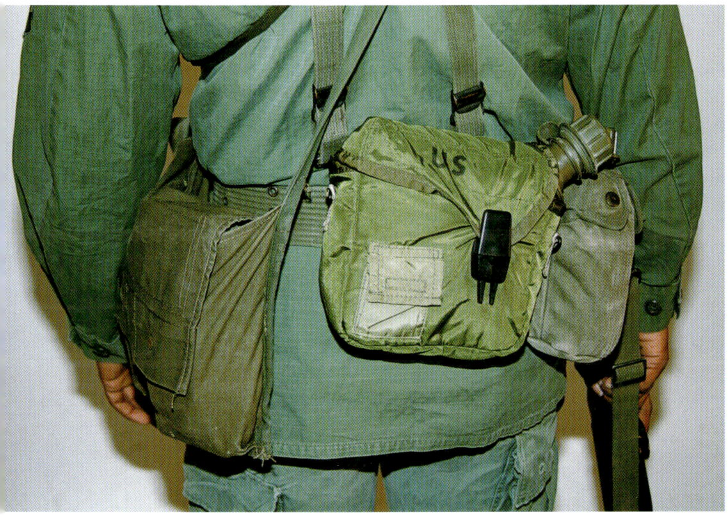

lose up showing the M1956 pistol belt with the second model nylon 2qt canteen over, which became available in 1968. Note the M18 Claymore mine bag.

Close up showing the upper torso of the grenadier gives a good view of the grenade bandoleer with the early solid snaps. Note also the matching name strip and U.S. Army tape, along with the hand sewn C.I.B.

Upper torso shot showing a 4th Infantry SSI, showing a combat tour with them.

cover that is Olive Green Army shade 106. The collapsible 2-quart canteen was introduced in 1967, while the cover seen here was the second model, and not readily available until late 1968. Attached to the left side of his H-harness is the angle head flashlight. Slung over his shoulder is the ever popular claymore mine bag that was often used as a "carry all, general-purpose bag."

Members of the 1st Cav move out during the beginning of "Operation Persh ing" in Bihn Dinh Province, Feb. 1968. Note the Playboy Bunny graffiti on th M-60 gunner's helmet.

This actually has the M18 mine inside, along with the wire an "clacker" firing device.

An additional six rounds of 40mm are carried in the cotto bandoleer seen here slung across his chest. Around his neck is th OD green triangular bandage that could be worn this way, or whil riding on top of the M113s could be worn over the mouth an nose to keep out dirt and dust.

Carried by this soldier is the M-79, affectionately called th "blooper" for the sound it made when the round left the chambe "Springfield Armory had begun development of this 40x46mn SR weapon in the early 1950s. A basic goal of the weapon wa the replacement of the standard rifle fired grenade, and 60mn mortar at the squad and platoon level. The M79 could cover th area between the longest range of the hand grenade (30-40meters and the middle range of the 60mm mortar (300-400meters). I the hands of a skilled grenadier, the M79 was highly accurate t 200 meters, and worked well in the jungle and in the building t building fighting of urban warfare. The M79's basic combat round the M-406, was a 170-grain high-explosive fragmentation gre

Sun, Dust, and wind goggles. These are the correct ones, and have a rough feel to the rubber. The post war goggles, 1974 to the present, feature a foam rubber padding along the rim that touches the face. The elastic strap DOES NOT go through the lens like the wartime ones due, and the newer ones are dated 1974. These are incorrect goggles for Vietnam.

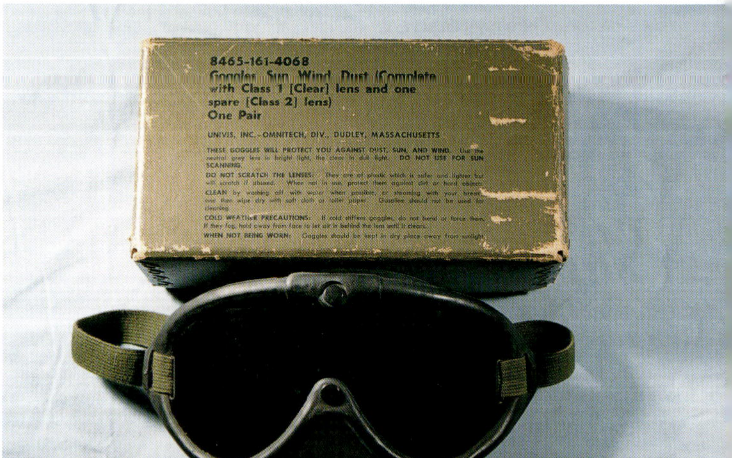

Close up of goggles with green issue box. Note the tinted lens, and the elasti straps go through the lens.

ull shot of LRP from the 58th Infantry. Note the 1965 Kodak camera in his left and and the obsolete German MP40 sub machine pistol.

Close up showing 101st Airborne patch. Note the tab is Vietnamese produced, while the actual patch is U.S. made. Also note the U.S. produced E-5 chevrons.

ade at a velocity of 76m/s per second to a maximum range of 00 meters. Development of the grenade-type warhead for the veapon that would become the M79 came out of the research onducted at the U.S. Army Ballistic Research Laboratories (BRL) t Aberdeen Proving Ground."

ompany F-58 Infantry (Airborne),
eam 10; 101st Airborne Division
amp Eagle, 1968
RRP

Worn by this recreated Company F-58th Infantry, Long-Range atroller in Nov. 1968 is a Vietnamese copy of the popular Army vaterproof parka. This one is fabricated from the standard nylon oated poncho with hood, olive green Army shade 207. Unlike he U.S. issue parka, this one has been lined with the camouflage oncho liner for added warmth during the cold monsoon season t Camp Eagle outside of Hue. On the left sleeve is the SSI of the 01st, along with a Vietnamese made E-5 chevron. Usually rank nsignia or SSI is not found on rain gear. Worn underneath is a set f the new ERDL fatigues in "rip-stop" cotton poplin. In his hand s a German MP 40 machine pistol, in 9mm.

Close up of the pocket guide to Vietnam that just about everybody received once they arrived in Vietnam.

Close up of right side showing a Vietnamese made 4th Infantry SSI.

Close up showing the poncho liner that has been added to the inside of the rai jacket for added warmth. Also note the florescent colors of the green dominan ERDL he is wearing.

Tom Newbauer, 4th Bn. 3d Inf. "Old Guard," 23d I.D. sits on a large granite boulder, with his M60 and "air-conditioned" trousers. Behind him the deadly "Heip Valley," NVA territory. (Tom Newbauer collection)

Tom Newbauer, right, and unidentified left, prepare to move out. Note the ma on the left has a subdued pocket patch of the 11th Light Infantry Brigade. Tom is seen here once again with only a T-shirt. (Tom Newbauer collection)

Good shot of both the ERDL uniform and the rain Jacket.

Mike O'Conner from D Company, 4th of the 3d Infantry, 11th (L.I.B), 23d Americal Div. (Courtesy Mike O'Conner)

Tom Newbauer prepares to move out. Note the lack of a shirt, the sleeveless T-shirt, and the old WWII era plywood pack-board. (Tom Newbauer collection)

Time off back in the rear. Note the aluminum cot frames, 1968. (Tom Newbauer collection)

Tom Newbauer prepares to move out through the grass as he lifts the heavy "Pig" onto his shoulder. Note the red bag in his helmet band. (Tom Newbauer collection)

Tom Newbauer "takes 5" to smoke a cigarette. (Tom Newbauer collection)

Tom Newbauer catches some "zzs" inside a makeshift hooch. Note the clean living conditions. (Tom Newbauer collection)

Tom Newbauer carves out a fighting position for the M60. Note the D ring on his trouser belt. (Tom Newbauer collection)

Tom Newbauer has just finished racing up the hill to engage some fleeing enemy soldiers. Note the man behind him has a large walking stick. (Tom Newbauer collection)

A very tired Mike O'Conner in his khaki uniform that was just pulled out of a duffel bag prepares to leave for home from Tan Son Nhut Airport. Note the two pocket hangers, the 23d on his left and the 11th LIB on his right, both in country made. Over his left shoulder is an item unique to the "Old Guard" that dates back to the War of 1812. (Mike O'Conner collection)

Left: *Close up of WWII era 23d SSI, note the khaki backing. These were still being issued in 1968.*

Below: *Close up 11th L.I.B. patch, usually worn on the right pocket and a Vietnamese made 23d Americal SSI. (Courtesy Mike O'Conner)*

Two examples of CIBs. Top is hand sewn, while the bottom one is machine made.

Example of Vietnamese made sewing kit.

2nd Battalion, 505th Infantry (Airborne) "Panthers,"
3d Brigade, 82nd Airborne Division
Hue/Phu Bai, 1968
RTO

"The paratrooper's steel pot is fitted with the M-1 Parachutist' liner. In 1966 the last variation of the M-1 Parachutist helm liner was produced. Existing production nylon helmet liners wer taken and modified to parachutist standards through the additio of female snap fasteners to receive the web chinstrap of the hel met body. The para helmet body required the addition of the body' extended web chin strap to existing production helmet bodies." Secured in the Band, Helmet, Camouflage are packs of Winsto cigarettes, a M16 speed loader, and pinned to the front, a pair o pin back airborne wings.

Uniform is the final version Jungle Fatigues produced in "Rip Stop" cotton poplin. Worn on the left sleeve is a WWII era on piece 82nd Airborne shoulder sleeve insignia (SSI). The 82n was one of the few units who never received a subdued "twill version of their colorful patch. Above his left pocket is a nylo U.S. Army strip, along with a basic parachute badge.

Sewing kit shown here opened with all the items still together. These could be bought just about anywhere.

Front view of 82nd Airborne RTO.

ide view showing RTO utilizing the PRC 77 radio. Note the plastic bag over he handset.

Left side gives a good view of both the new short M16 pouches and the newer nylon canteen cover.

Web gear consists of a cotton H-harness connected to a M1966 "vertical weave" pistol belt that features the "Davis" quick release fastener, which received mixed reviews. Attached are two of the newer canvas Small Arms Ammunition Cases, M16A1 20 round. These were first introduced in 1968, and were designed especially for the 20 round magazine. Attached are two M-26 Hand-grenades. Worn on either side of the ammo pouches are two of the M1967 nylon canteen carriers with plastic snap.

The PRC 77 Radio, an improved version of the PRC-25 radio having a completely solid state design that provided more reliability while requiring less power, is carried on the aluminum pack-board attachment. The aluminum pack-board came with two nylon quick release strap and clamp assemblies, used to secure the radio and other items to the aluminum frame. Attached to the radio is the RTO's poncho, along with a VA-17 marker panel, which is folded inside the poncho. A piece of 550 "para" cord is tied to the radio and used to carry a single 1 qt. Canteen, three M-18 smoke grenades, an M17 mask and its carrier, spare part bag, and an additional 2qt canteen. The radio handset has been placed

Close up showing the OD green issue towel that this paratrooper is wearing around his neck.

Back view shows the radio, along with numerous smoke grenades, an M17 gas mask, and a 2qt canteen. Note the pop flare in his right pocket.

Typical well faded Vietnamese made boonie hats in the "Fedora" style. This boonie hat started out OG green, but has since faded to a sandy brown. Directly embroidered to the crown are the words Viet-Nam, along with the years 1968-1969. Also on the brim (going clockwise) are 81mm, indicating the owner is a mortarman, Gypsies in Viet-Nam, indicating he was mechanized, RPPB, and finally, E. Co. The 101st patch in the center is a Vietnamese made one piece variation.

in the plastic bag that held the dry-cell battery, used here to keep moisture out during the monsoon season. Note that when the handset is not in use, it is stuffed inside the RTO's right breast pocket. Around his neck is an OD green towel. Note the single pop-flare in his right trouser cargo pocket, which could be used for signaling.

Close up of XM28 lightweight protective mask and its nylon carrier. These began arriving in Vietnam in 1967, but were not used in great numbers until late '68-early '69 when they became plentiful.

Front of boonie hat showing a crude Vietnamese made C.I.B. and the letters R.P.P.B.

Close up of third and final model OG 107 cotton sateen shirt. This one belonged to a 1st LT. in the newly arrived 1st Brigade of the 5th Infantry Division.

Troops from the 5th Bn. of the 7th Cavalry and crews take a break along a road in South Vietnam. Note the helicopters and the O-1 Bird Dog Observation plane.

Left side showing U.S. made 5th Infantry SSI.

Full right side showing a nice twill 9th Inf. Div. SSI showing a combat tour with them.

Probably one of the smallest aircraft carriers, this ATC is equipped with a deck big enough to land a UH-1H helicopter. These came in handy in emergencies when Medivacs had no where to land to evacuate the wounded. The majority of men on the ATC seen here are all Navy. Note most are wearing tennis shoes. (U.S. Army photo)

Full front shot showing the entire shirt. Note the C.I.B. is U.S. made.

5

1969

1st Battalion, 7th Cavalry, 1st Cavalry Division "Flowing Vengeance," 1969 Pointman

Worn on the left sleeve of this Pointman is a U.S. made twill 1st Cav. Patch. Below, worn on both sleeves, are U.S. produced E-4, Corporal chevrons, something very uncommon in Vietnam. Worn on his "combat" side is a twill 25th Infantry SSI, showing a combat tour with the "Tropic Lighting" Division. Although unseen, worn above his U.S. Army strip is a Vietnam made C.I.B.

Web gear worn by this point man consists of a cotton M1956 web belt with two universal pouches, each containing extra rounds for his shotgun. Two M26 grenades are fastened to the inside of the pouches. Secured to his right universal pouch is a twin cell ammunition pouch for his .45 cal auto pistol. Connected to his H-harness are a single caribiner and a compass pouch, in which he

Members of the 2nd Battalion, 60th Infantry, 9th Infantry Division Tan Tru, 1969.

Full figure of Point man 1st Cavalry, 1969.

Another full figure of point-man.

Full rear shot of point-man. Note the lightweight rucksack connected to the top of the frame.

has secured his plastic C Rat spoon. Slung across his chest is the newer nylon carrier for the two-quart collapsible canteen. Worn on the rear of the pistol belt is the M1961 butt pack containing a poncho-liner and a day's rations. The lightweight rucksack is seen here with its nylon bag secured to the top of its aluminum frame. The Lightweight ruck could accommodate twice as much as the M1961 buttpack, was water repellent, and featured double eyelet web tabs for the attachment of other items, such as a 1qt canteen with cover, seen here.

Secured under his ruck is the "standard heavy weight nylon coated poncho with hood, Olive Green Army shade 207, which was adopted in 1961."[42] A "USARV Tropical Combat Uniform Board reported in 1965 that the poncho was inadequate for Vietnam, since it became relatively heavy when wet and had a shiny finish that gleamed in the rain. Natick Labs developed a new lightweight poncho on 14 Feb. 1966."[43]

The new lightweight poncho weighed half as much as the M1961 poncho, but many preferred the water repellency of the old style to the weight difference.

Attached to his shotgun is a modified G.P. "general purpose" sling with the addition of elastic material to hold numerous shotgun rounds in place. The shotgun was reliable, lightweight, and dependable, and very sought after in Vietnam by pointmen and others alike. Two additional shotgun rounds are secured in his helmet band.

'lose up of right side showing U.S. produced twill 25th patch on his combat 'ide. Note the GP strap with additional shotgun rounds.

Close up of the left side with emphasis on his mid section. Note the twill U.S. manufactured 1st Cavalry SSI. Also note the U.S. made E-4 corporal stripes, a rare item.

'pper torso close up showing ıe shotgun, along with a good iew of the locally adapted 'hotgun sling. Note the additional shotgun rounds inside his elmet band.

Close up showing much of the point-man's Load Bearing Equipment.

Close up showing the Lightweight rucksack. Note the poncho secured to the bottom of the ruck, just above his M1961 buttpack.

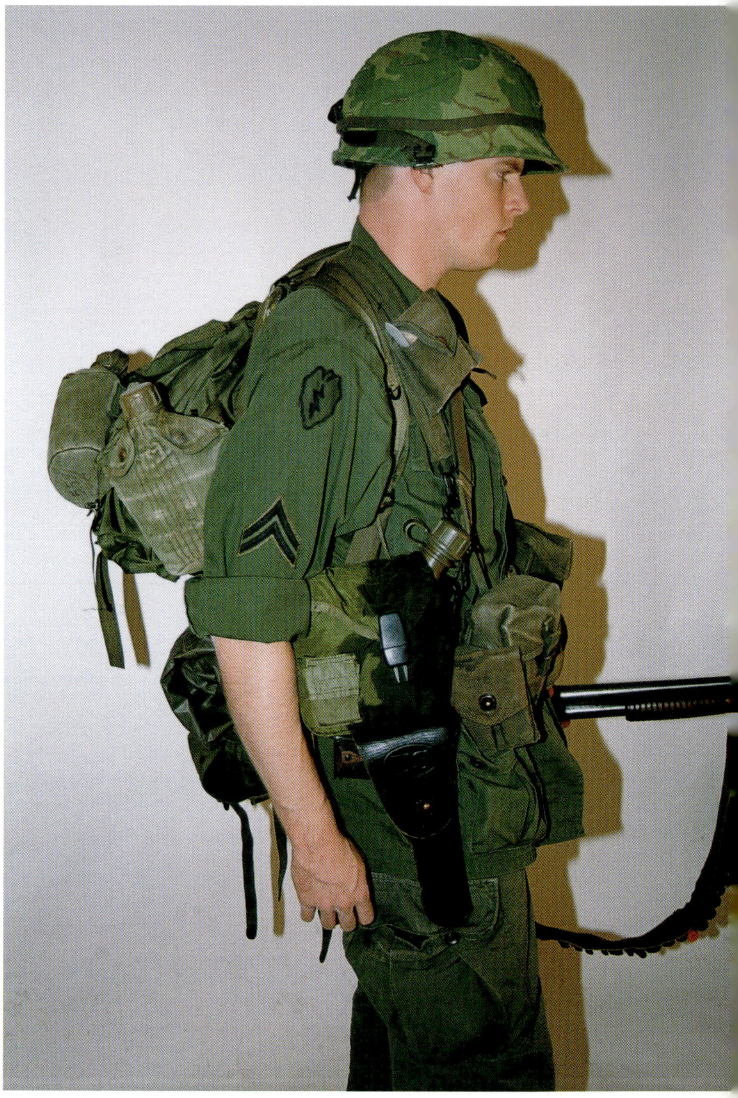

Close up showing right side allows a good view of his pistol, and note the odd place he has chosen to secure his twin cell magazine pouch for his .45 pistol connected to his universal pouch. Also note the white plastic spoon in his first aid/compass pouch.

Close up of Vietnamese made C.I.B.

Typical envelope provided for all servicemen serving in Vietnam. No stamp was necessary, all out going mail was free!

Close up showing a $5.00 bill in Government Payment Certificate. Servicemen were paid in this "funny money" to keep American "Green Backs" off the black market.

Rear view of Pointman. Note the color of the backside of his holster, showing it was once tan and has since been dyed black

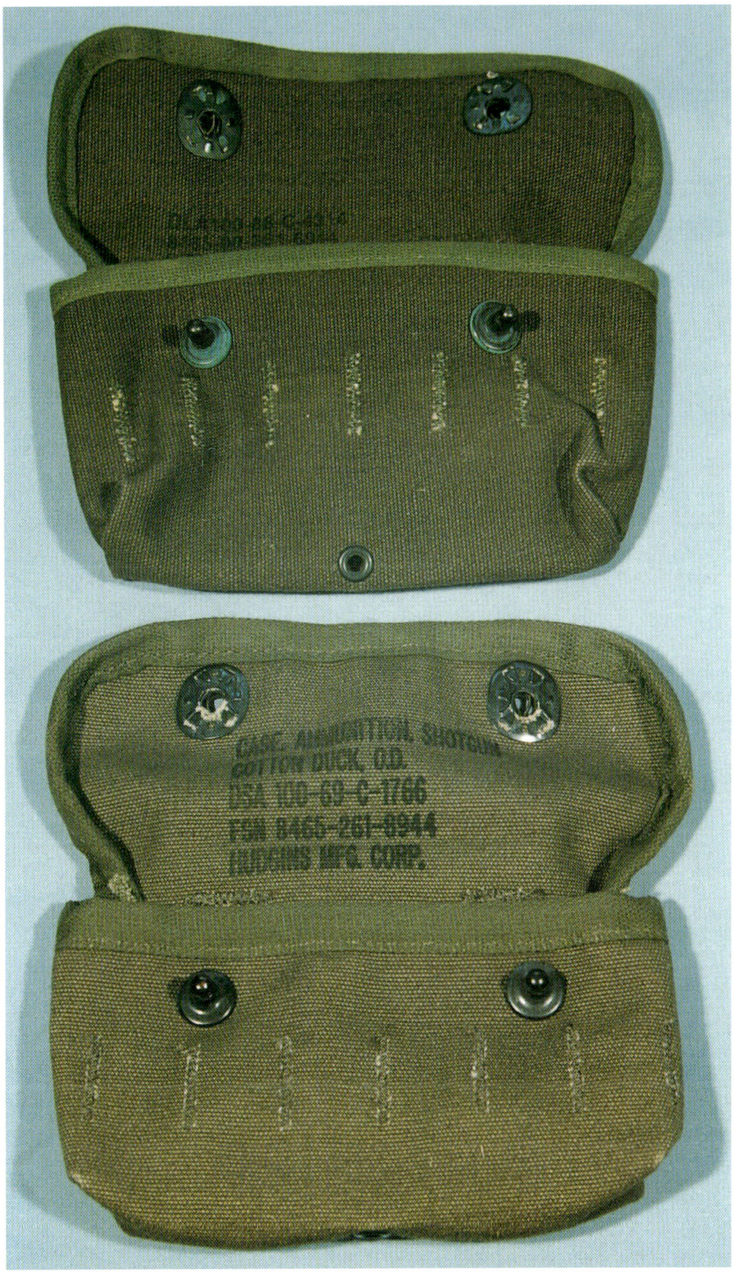

Close up showing the Shotgun pouch that was available and sometimes issued in sets along with the shotgun. These were rarely seen, and men armed with shotguns had to come up with ways of holding the rounds. (Top) modern day 1988 version of the Case, Ammunition, Shotgun, Cotton Duck OD, and (Bottom) DSA-100-69-C-1766 shows that this case was produced in 1969. Note the two are very much alike, except the make stamp is quite small on the top modern one and is slightly darker OD green.

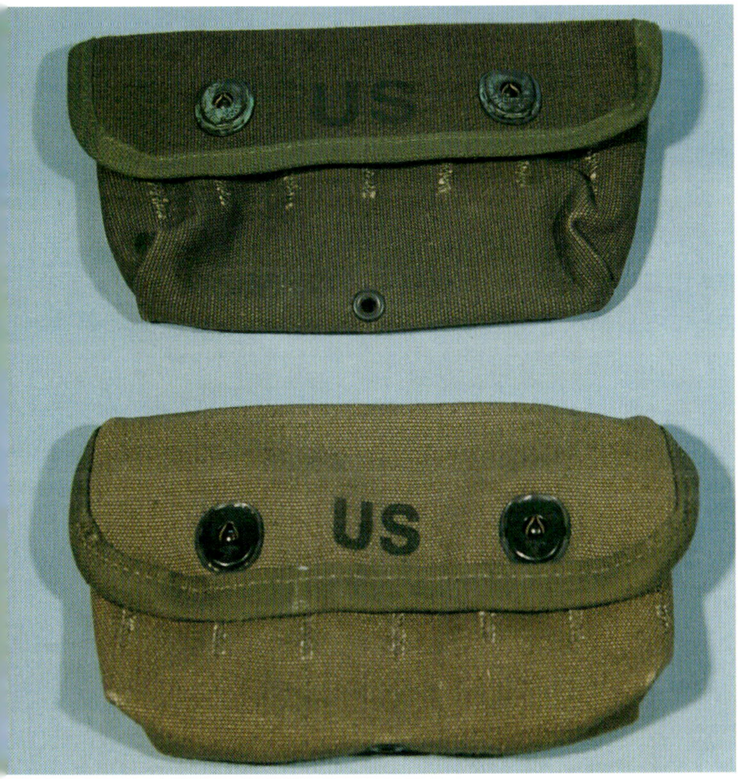

Left: *Close up of the two shotgun cases (Top) Modern, (Bottom) Vietnam era. Note that when closed, the two are very hard to tell apart other than the differences in color, along with the cotton trim along the border of the flap. Both can be secured to the pistol belt by a set of belt loops on the rear.*

Company Commander of Alpha Company, 1st Battalion, 52nd Infantry in Bong Son, 1969.

Full Figure of Company Commander with map and compass.

Close up of the CO's head and shoulders. Note he wears the M1 helmet with the Fall/Winter brown side of his helmet cover, along with a Vietnamese made (0-3) Captain bars sewn to the front.

1st Battalion, 52nd Infantry,
23rd Infantry; "Americal Division"
Song Bon River, 1969
Company Commander

"The Army's standard combat helmet of the Vietnam War was the M1 steel helmet, which rendered the wearer protection against flying shrapnel and ricocheting bullets."[44] "The cloth helmet cover was printed with a disruptive camouflage pattern using selected organic dyes and resin-bonded pigments. This was a 'duotone' reversible cover in both green (spring) and brown (Fall/Winter)." Worn here is the Fall/Winter side with a Vietnamese produced cloth Capt. bars hastily sewn onto it. Secured in his helmet band camouflage is a single book of matches.

"Rip-stop" cotton jungle fatigues were common by 1969, though it was not uncommon to find soldiers wearing mismatched sets of cotton/cotton "rip-stop" combined. Worn on his left shoulder is a crude 23rd Americal SSI, "Southern Cross," which were available throughout the country. A single woven U.S. Army strip

Close up showing the CO's midsection. Note the new M1967 1QT nylon canteen cover.

Close up showing the Vietnamese made 23d "Americal" SSI. Note the dark green material used.

Close up showing the Captain. Note the subdued pin on rank and BOS; Infantry, worn on his collar points. The 550 cord attached to the right side of his H-harness is used to secure his compass.

Close up showing issue rank (O-3) Captain. Note the date, 1969.

Close up of the left side of the Company Commander. On his belt he wears the new XM28 Lightweight Protective mask in its nylon carrier. He also has an older universal pouch, evident by the grommet. Note the "Skillcraft" pen in his pocket, these are almost identical to the U.S. Government Skillcraft pens used today. The only difference is the new one features two black rings on the silver band located on the center of the pen.

Full figure shot of the right side of the Company Commander.

is worn parallel to the pocket, which became predominant by 1969. Note that on his right side his name has been written on with a black felt marker, "Hopkins." Pin on subdued Branch Of Service (BOS), Infantry crossed rifles and Captain bars are worn on his collar points.

Worn on his M1956 pistol belt is the new "XM28 Lightweight protective Mask. The 13-ounce mask has a vinyl, waterproof carrier, which could be fitted into the Tropical Combat uniform's trouser cargo pocket."[45] Just to the left of his mask is an early model universal pouch, which featured the grommet in the tab. Next to that is the M1967 nylon canteen cover, which featured plastic snaps and a small pocket for the water purification bottle. On his right side is the first aid/compass pouch, an additional universal pouch, and the black leather holster for his .45 cal. Colt auto pistol. Secured to the right side of his H-harness is the "magnetic lensatic compass, which was used to establish direction. An accurate line of direction could be established for a specific object by using the arrangement of a lensatic eyelens, a sight line,

Close up of the Capt.'s left side gives a good view of his other M1967 nylon 1QT-canteen cover.

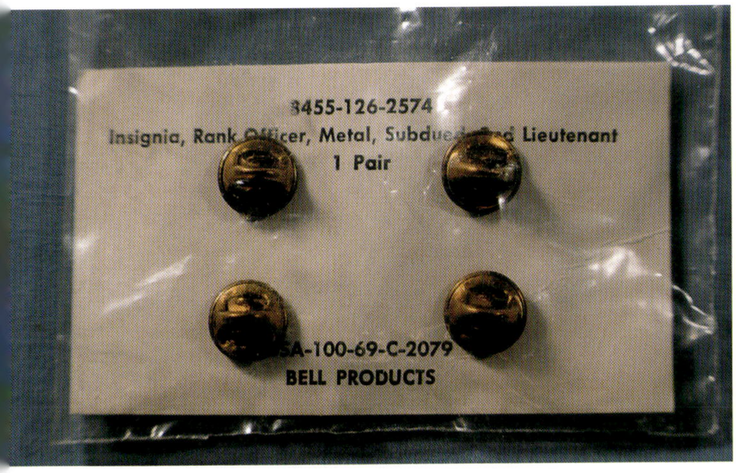

Close up showing Insignia, Rank Officer, Metal, Subdued, 2nd Lieutenant. Dated 1969.

and the object being sighted." The compass is seen tied with 550 cord, sometimes referred to as "dummy cord." Below that is his angle head flashlight. Around his waist is worn a single M-16 bandoleer with seven 20-round magazines for his M16A1 rifle.

Pathfinder Detachment,
25th Infantry Division,
Cu Chi, 1969.

"Pathfinder organization was extremely flexible, with the basic element being the four-man pathfinder team. Three or more teams, depending on the size of the mission of the supported aviation unit, comprised a Pathfinder Detachment. Detachments were attached to aviation units on an as needed basis, and though they had their own numerical designation, were usually known by that or their parent aviation battalion or group, i.e. 25th Pathfinder Det. By 1972 when the U.S. withdrew from Vietnam there were 26 teams, along with various provisional, sections, detachments, and platoons. They were usually authorized 16 men in three four-man Pathfinder Teams and a four man HQ, also capable of functioning as a team. It was not unusual for these detachments to be unmanned or at greatly reduced strengths. Besides clearing LZs, Pathfinders could and routinely served as Rescue and Recovery of downed aircraft, helicopters, and their crews, then rigged them for extraction by helicopter, secured helicopter landing zones, and directed artillery and helicopter gunship fire support. Though of-

Full figure of 25th Infantry "Pathfinder."

Full figure shot of Tropic Lighting Pathfinder, with emphasis on the right/rear. Note the SDU-5/E strobe light in its nylon carrier sewn directly to the 1qt M1956 canteen cover.

Full shot providing a good look at his large subdued World War II "style" pathfinder badge worn on the left pocket flap of his Transitional pattern ERDL shirt. Note also his nylon M1967 canteen cover being used to hold 20 round magazines for his CAR-15.

Left side of Pathfinder, showing the locally made Pathfinder scroll and U.S. made twill SSI of the 25th Infantry Division.

ten misused or under-employed—a common occurrence in the U.S. Army for small, specialized units—the Pathfinders in Vietnam performed a valuable and much needed service in a combat environment so dependent on the helicopter for transport, fire support, and re-supply."[46]

This re-creation is typical of a member of a four-man team serving with the 25th Inf. Div. in 1969. This Asst. team leader wears the "transitional pattern" of ERDL, being neither the brown dominant "Highland pattern" nor the green dominant "Lowland" pattern. First introduced in or around 1968-69, the camo pattern differs from the traditional pattern in the colors and shapes used. The pattern closely resembles the post war pattern sometimes called the Rapid Deployment Force (RDF) camo. Contrary to the way in which the outline of the pattern is visible from the inside of the ERDL, the transitional pattern inside has a spotty white on green, which is very distinctive. All three forms of the Army's ERDL pattern uniforms quickly gained high acceptability, despite the tendency they had to tear while worn on patrols in Vietnam's dense jungles. The lighter material was lighter and much more comfortable than the indigenous camouflage clothing. Worn above his twill 25th SSI is a locally made Pathfinder scroll. Worn over his pocket flaps are locally produced name and U.S. Army strips. Above his U.S. Army is a pair of basic parachute qualification

C Company's Commander, Capt. Suazo, wearing a white RANGER shirt, stands in front of Company sign in 1969. Behind him is a small guidon that reads "Killers."

Front of Pathfinder provides a view of his LBE. Note he wears no H-harness with his pistol belt.

Spc. 4 Craig Smith, C. Company, 1st Bn (AMBL), 501st INF. wears a ripstop set of Jungle fatigues in 1969. Note the BCG (Birth Control Glasses) and clean M16. (C. Smith/L. Martin Collection)

C. Smith, 1-501st INF and men of C. Company in the field. The man far left wears a boonie under his helmet and wears an early model pistol belt with the prototype Davis buckle. The man next to him holds a shotgun and has several of the new "baseball" grenades. The man on the far right has two 20 round magazines taped together, along with an XM28 Lightweight Protective mask on his pistol belt. (C. Smith/ L. Martin collection)

wings. Worn on his left pocket is the pre-1969 Pathfinder qualification badge; in the months to come it will be reduced to the same size as the airborne wings and worn in conjunction with other qualification badges, above the pocket. Around his neck is a pair of the Sun, Wind, and Dust goggles, with the tinted lenses, which were used to keep flying debris out of his eyes during operations. A single M1967 canteen cover is used in lieu of an ammunition case, along with a new M16 ammo pouch in canvas. Sewn to the outside of his M1956 canteen cover is the SDU/5/E strobe light distress marker in its nylon case. Two Red M18 smoke grenades are connected to the back of his PRC/77 radio on its carrying harness, along with the bag containing the spare antennas and handset, which is also attached to the harness. "The headset with internal boom type microphone is part of the 'hands free' system, which eliminated the need for the handset. The unit that houses the transmit section switch (featuring intermittent or continuous 'talk' modes) is suspended on the chest by a neck harness."[47] "The XM177 or CAR-15 (Colt Automatic Rifle) was the sub-machine gun version of the M16. Shorter and lighter, with a telescoping stock, the CAR-15 was favored by recon type personnel and anyone else who could get their hands on one."[48] Headgear is a locally produced tigerstripe beret.

C Company, 1st Battalion, 501st Infantry (Airborne), 101st (Airmobile)
Phu Bai, 1969.
RTO

Worn on the left sleeve of this paratrooper is a full color U.S. made SSI of the 101st. "Units like the 101st, which exhibited intense pride in its fiercely colorful 'Screaming Eagle' patch, blatantly ignored the regulations in Vietnam that all patches must be

Unidentified soldier from the 1st Bn., 501st Infantry. Note the full color 101st SSI, Van Xa Vietnam, 1969. (C. Smith/L. Martin Collection)

Several men from the 501st on top of clearing, all 5 wear ripstop jungle fatigues. Note the strange boonie hat on the man kneeling, and the sleeve-less T-shirt on the man second on the left. Craig Smith is the man on the far left. (C. Smith/L. Martin Collection)

Full figure of 1st Bn. 501st Infantry, 101st (AMBL) 1969.

subdued, and was one of the very few patches that were not mad in the subdued variation."[49] The "Screaming Eagle" is a U.S. produced item, while the "Airborne" arc is locally produced, as evident by the color and the crudeness. Both his U.S. Army and nam strip are worn parallel to the pockets, which became the norm on 5 Sept 1969. "In July of 1967, the USARV concurred with the adoption of subdued pin on metal insignia of rank for enliste men, in lieu of sew on cloth rank. A year later, the Army authorized worldwide wear of this device on all duty uniforms."[50] Worn here are SPC 4 sleeve rank, which are a locally produced variation and have begun to turn khaki tan. Worn above his U.S. Army strip is a Vietnamese made C.I.B.

Two men from the 501st, 101st (AMBL) stand shirtless in LZ with a green M18 smoke grenade. (C. Smith/ L. Martin Collection)

'ull figure with emphasis on his right side. This provides a good view of the ıelmet graffiti and his private purchase knife in its dark brown scabbard, which s secured to his trouser belt. Note the hand mike secured in plastic to keep out noisture.

Rear view of 101st soldier shows the PRC-77 connected to the frame with the small nylon bag of the lightweight ruck behind it. This gives the RTO more room inside his ruck. Note the 2qt canteen and cover, two M18 smoke grenades, and the XM28 Lightweight Protective mask in its nylon carrier secured to his ruck.

Minimal web gear is carried by this RTO, as evidenced by this photo. Pistol belt minus the cotton H-harness is worn with two universal pouches, and two M1956 canteen covers, in which one is being used to hold additional M16 magazines. Secured to the universal pouch on the right is a single M26 grenade, while on the right is a White Smoke grenade.

Worn on his trouser belt, just barely visible is a Western hunting knife, sent over from home, in a brown leather scabbard. Attached to his left side of the Light Weight ruck is the new nylon water repellent cover for the LP (Limited Production) Bladder, 2-quart canteen, which was made of a vinyl acetate copolymer (plastic). These nylon covers were first produced in 1968, and featured a small pocket for a water-purification bottle, as well as a removable sling and slide lock fasteners to attach it to the ruck or pistol belt. Although the canteen was standardized in early 1967, they saw limited use, and these covers did not see service until late 68 or early 69. Directly behind the 2qt and cover is the Spare Parts Bag for the PRC-25 Radio. In it would most likely be an additional handset, long antenna, base for the long antenna, and possibly an additional short 'tape' antenna. On the opposite side is a M1956 canteen cover with a 1qt plastic canteen, along with

Craig Smith, "Shorty," and a few men from the CQ office clown around during some down time. Note the model boats and helos in the back. (C. Smith/ L. Martin collection)

Front view of 101st soldier.

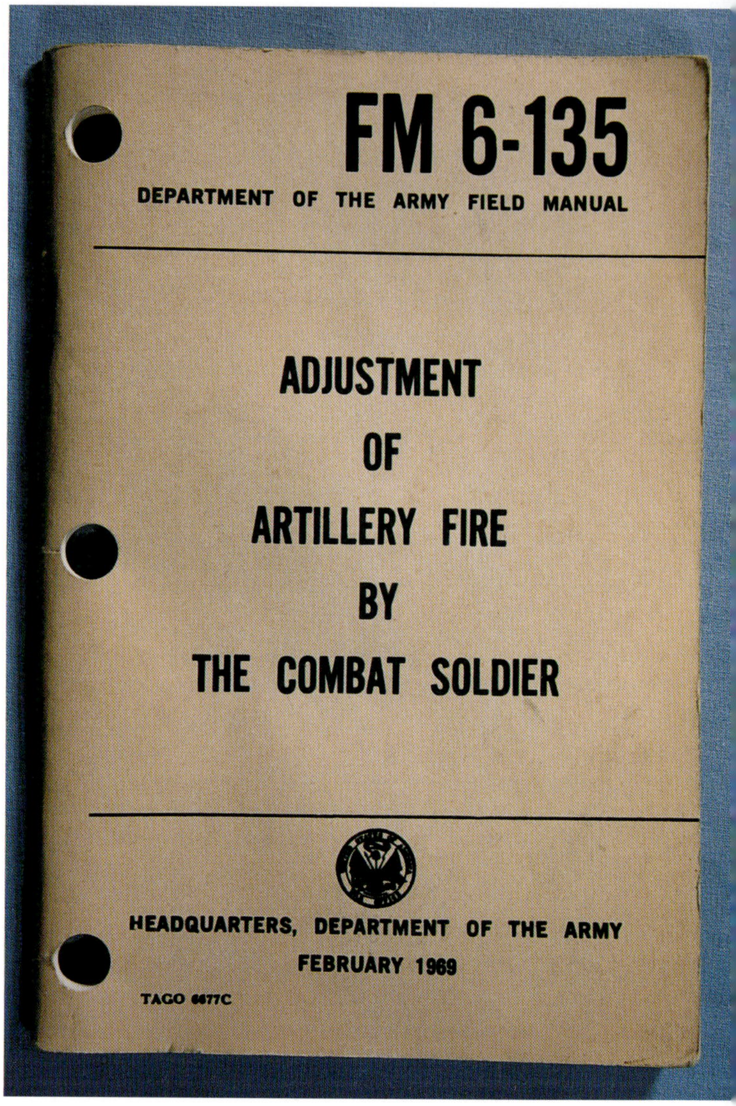

Close up of FM 6-135 Adjustment of Artillery dated 1969.

the new XM28 Lightweight protective mask in its nylon carrier. Connected to the center of the ruck are two M18 smoke grenades.

The camouflage helmet cover would remain unchanged until 1969, when a new pattern much like the ERDL was adopted, although it saw limited use in Vietnam. Drawn on the helmet cover is a 101st SSI with the words "VC can be cured, the prescription: the 101st 'Airmobile.'" Secured inside the Band, Helmet, Camouflage, is a single bottle of "bug juice." The chin strap is worn in the typical fashion, in the helmet band instead of under the chin!

The PRC/25 is seen here attached to the Lightweight rucksack frame, instead of carried inside the small nylon bag. This left more room for personal items, as well as batteries, night vision device (AN/PVS-2 scope), mortar rounds, additional bandoleers of ammo, and water! "The AN/PRC-25 was a short-range man pack portable, frequency modulated (FM) receiver/transmitter, weighing just over 24 pounds with the dry cell battery. Each battery had an average life of about 20 hours. Maximum range for the radio was from 5KM with the short tape antenna and up to 8km with the long seven section "fish pole" antenna. The radio was part valve/part transistor and had 920 channels, in which two were pre-set."[51] Note the plastic bag over the hand mike.

Men from the 501st set up a hasty C.P. in the woods during operations, 1969. (C. Smith/L. Martin Collection)

Craig Smith (Far Right) and other members of C Company 1st Bn, 501st Inf. Note Craig Smith wears the brim only of an OD bush hat, the top has been completely removed. (C. Smith/ L. Martin collection)

Craig Smith (Left) and unidentified sit on a cot in their "Hooch." Note the bamboo floor mat and the Simon & Garfunkel poster on the wall behind Craig. (C. Smith/ L. Martin Collection)

Craig Smith (Right) with his boots off in his fighting position. Note the makeshift shelter the two have constructed and the Pepsi® can in between the two—all the comforts of home! 1969. (C. Smith/L. Martin Collection)

Four members of Company C 1st Bn., 501st Inf. show off exotic weapons. The man at the far left has an M-3 "Grease gun," the man in the back (sitting) holds a WWII shotgun with a ventilated barrel and bayonet lug, C. Smith (far right) holds an M-79, and the man with the sunglasses has an M16 rifle. (C. Smith/L. Martin Collection)

Full figure of Medic from the 6th Bn., 31st Infantry, 9th Infantry Division, Ben Luc, 1969.

Rear view of Medic. Note the 2qt canteen with D-ring secured to the frame of his Lightweight rucksack. Also note his cargo pockets are full of extra bandages.

6th Battalion, 31st Infantry, "The Polar Bears"
9th Infantry Division.
Ben Luc, 1969
Medic

This medic wears the new rip-stop jungle fatigues, which were basically cotton-poplin, which incorporated a nylon weave that greatly increased the strength of the fabric. The only patch worn is a crude 9th Infantry Division, worn on the left sleeve of his "rip-stop" poplin shirt. "The 'Octofoil' shoulder insignia represented the heraldic symbol of the 9th son and was referred to as the psychedelic cookie."[52] Worn where his U.S. Army strip would be is his Vietnamese made sandcast Combat Medical Badge. The badge was awarded to signify excellence in duty performed under hazardous conditions and in circumstances of extraordinary hardship. The CMB was very coveted, much like the CIB for Infantrymen. It was not uncommon to see soldiers in uniforms with absolutely no insignia at all.

Close up showing the silver Vietnamese made Combat Medical Badge (C.M.B.), and the crudely made 9th Infantry Division patch. Note the lack of a helmet band on his M1 steel pot.

Full figure shot with emphasis on the Medics right side. Note the "Unit 1" aid bag.

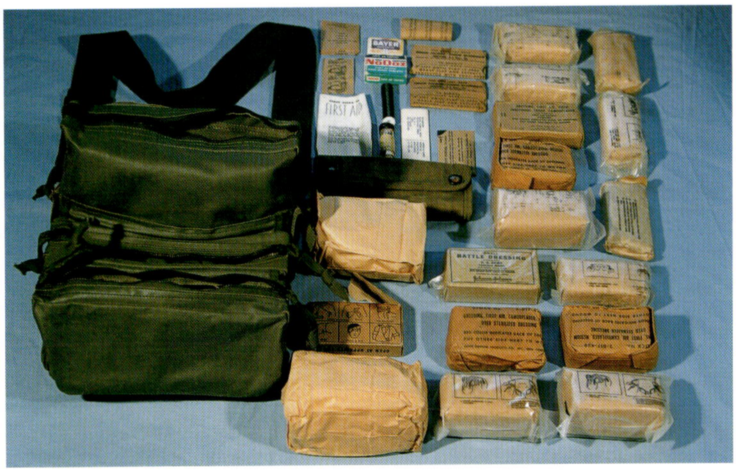

Close up showing the contents of his Unit-1 bag. Note that some of the dressings are WWII vintage. Also note the civilian NO DOZ and Bayer aspirin (middle top)

Worn slung over his shoulder is the post-68 model Aid bag with a distinct grey-green rubberized coating much like the one used for the 67 pattern 2-quart canteen cover. The bag was identical to the Korean War era one, except for the rubberized cover, and featured the exact same space allotment for bandages and medical supplies. The case, medical instrument and supply set, non-rigid, number 3, better known as the "aid bag," was carried by all field medical personnel and was filled with supplies according to mission requirements. Typically, these kits contained: bandages, dressings, Vaseline gauze, instrument set, field medical cards, aspirin, antimalarial pills, antihistamine, salt tablets, water purification tablets, bacitracin, and tetracaine ointments, and Gelusil, along with cough medicine and adhesive strips. Still in evidence were components of World War II and Korean War era kits. The pouches for these kits were relegated to service as general-purpose containers for miscellaneous medical supplies.

"Ranges of blood-volume expanders and infusion sets were also available. Glass bottles of normal saline, Ringers' lactate

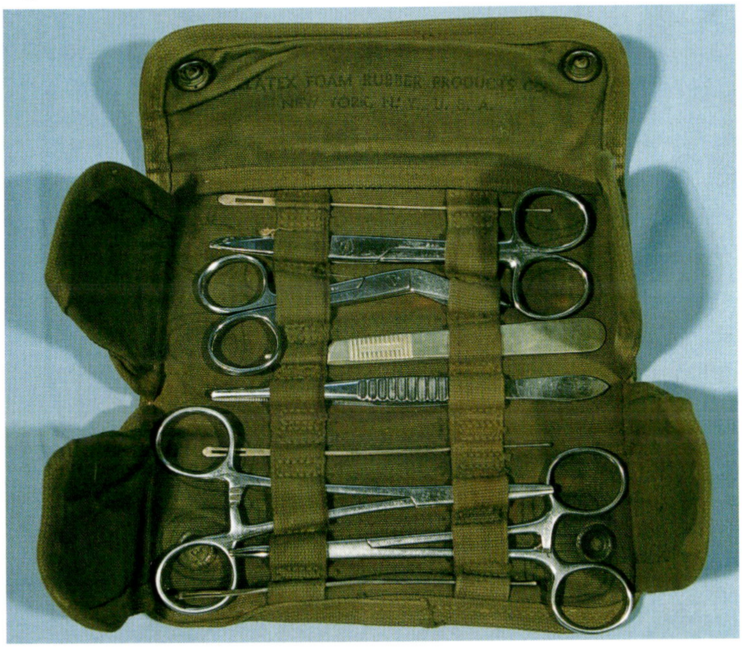

Close up showing the medical instrument set. Hard to see, but under each instrument is a diagram of it drawn on the canvas case.

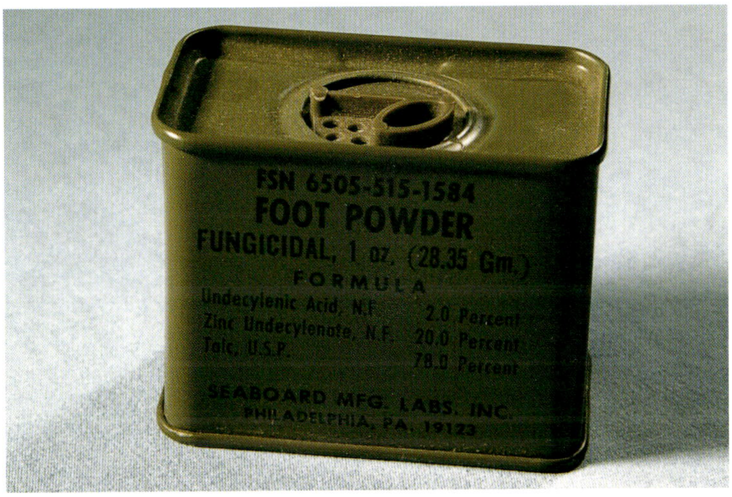

Close up of foot powder.

Full figure of "Indiana Ranger" Company D, 1st Field Force, Vietnam, 1969. Note the Mark V British Sten gun and the khaki Chi-Com vest.

Left side of Ranger. Note the 3-pocket pouch intended to hold magazines for the grease gun and sometimes the Tommy gun, but used here to hold the magazines for his British Sten gun. Also note the 2qt canteen and cover on the rear of his pistol belt.

solution, and plasmanate were often carried in canteen covers on the pistol belt."[53]

No LBE is worn, instead the medic carries everything needed for an extended mission inside his Lightweight rucksack. Connected to the top of the frame is a single two-quart canteen on a D-ring minus the cover, a common practice in the 9th Infantry Division. Worn around his waist is a cotton M16 bandoleer. Weapon is an M16 rifle, which was not an uncommon thing for medics to carry at this time.

Company D, LRRP "Indiana Rangers"
First Field Force Vietnam
Long Bihn, 1969
Ranger

"Co. D Long Range Patrol of the 151st Infantry had the distinct honor of being the only National Guardsmen volunteered for duty in S.E. Asia, and the Army agreed to omit it from infusion of outside personnel in order to maintain unit integrity. Before the guardsmen were sent overseas, they first had to complete an extensive 6 month training program sponsored by the Army Infantry school at Ft. Benning. They received specialized instruction and earned their Airborne wings. Some personnel were sent to the school of the Americas in the Panama Canal Zone and were jungle expert qualified at J.O.T.C. All this set the foundation for an exceptionally battle worthy long Range Patrol Company. At the end of Dec. 1968 the Rangers were flown to Vietnam and based at the former

Mark V Sten gun with several 9mm magazines inside the khaki Chi-Com AK 47 chest pouch, sometimes called an "apron."

'lose up, upper torso of Ranger. Underneath his H-harness are sewn an U.S. .rmy strip, airborne wings, and C.I.B., items usually not found on tigerstripe niforms. Note also the short brim tigerstripe boonie hat in the South Vietnamese 1arine Corps pattern.

On the left sleeve is a Vietnamese made "Kit Carson Scout" scroll with a matching Vietnamese made 23d Inf. Div. SSI. On the right side is a single name strip, LAM.

Hawk missile battery site at Camp Frenzell-Jones in Long Binh. The Company then underwent a week long Vietnam familiarization course along with the 199th Infantry Brigade, then received an additional 4 weeks of training set up by Company F, 51st LRRP."[54]

Worn across this Indiana Rangers' chest is the khaki tan Chi-Com AK-47 pouch, which could accommodate 4 long magazines in each of its three large pockets. Shown here in one of the pockets is a pop flare. The smaller pockets are the perfect size for the M-26 hand grenades and the M-18 smoke grenade. Once again, tigerstripe fatigues have been chosen over the newer U.S. ERDL camouflage. Although they featured fewer pockets than the U.S. fatigues, the Asian made tigers blended well with the jungle at night, and the "old

Close-up of khaki tan Chi-Com AK-47 pouch with numerous Mark V Sten gun magazines. These magazines were hard to obtain, and were very coveted. Note the M-18 smoke grenade secured in the small pocket, and the pop flare in the larger pockets.

Left: *Close up of typical 3d model Jungle jacket in "rip-stop" cotton poplin. Note the U.S. twill 9th Inf. Div. SSI and the locally produced E-6 chevrons.*

hands," the men with experience, had them. LBE consists of two universal pouches, each with several boxes of 9mm ammo, which is hard to obtain, and a single 1 qt. Canteen with cover, which would indicate a short screening mission that may only last 1-2 days. Connected to his H-harness on the left is a single D-ring. On his left side is the canvas first aid/compass pouch worn upside down with the blood type written on it. The headgear that became synonymous with the LRRPs and Rangers was the "boonie hat" worn here. These low crown hats with their semi-stiff brim could be molded or shaped to individual taste, resulting in a large variety of styles. This one is in the Vietnamese tigerstripe pattern. Around his neck is the OD green drive on rag. Weapon is the WWII vintage Mark V Sten gun, which weighs 8.7 lbs., was capable of both full and semi-automatic fire, had an effective range of 150 meters, and was a rugged and reliable weapon.

1st Battalion, 5th Infantry (Mechanized Infantry), 2d Brigade, 25th Infantry Division
Cu Chi, 1969
Rifleman

"Headgear worn by this Mechanized Infantryman is the boonie hat, which became synonymous with the Vietnam War. The Hat Jungle W/ Insect Net, was made out of 'rip-stop' cotton poplin, but were initially produced in cotton poplin. The hat features a wide brim, ventilation eyelets, chin strap, and foliage loops for attaching grenade pins."[55]

Uniform consists of cotton "rip-stop" shirt and trousers with a single U.S. twill SSI "Tropic Lightning" patch on his left shoulder. A motley collection of web gear is worn here by this trooper. A well-worn cotton H harness is connected to an M1956 pistol belt with two universal pouches in the front. Suspended from the right pouch is a D ring with a single 1qt plastic canteen. Draped over his web belt is a belt of M-60, 7.62 ammo. An additional universal pouch is worn on his right hip containing a single M18 smoke grenade, with a second one secured to the slot provided

Right: *Right side of jacket shows a full color 9th Inf. Div patch, showing a combat tour with the 9th Infantry Division a year before, probably in 1967.*

Full figure shot of 25th Infantry soldier.

Upper torso shot of 25th Infantry (Mechanized)

Rear shot showing the new camouflage poncho secured underneath his M1961 buttpack. Note the popflare secured along with the camouflage poncho.

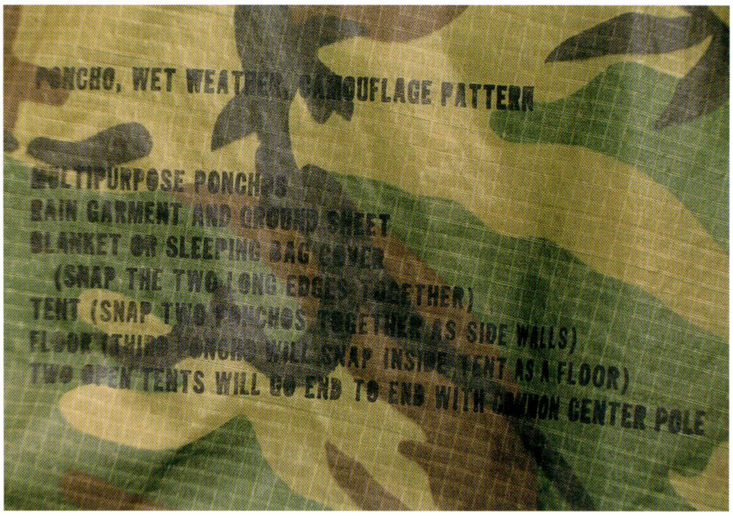

Close up of printed tag on camouflage poncho.

Right side of soldier. Note the extra universal pouch being used to carry an M1 smoke grenade. Also note the 1qt canteen on the D ring secured to the grena slot of his universal pouch.

for grenades, and safe-guarded with the web strap. The butt pack worn here is the larger, improved M1961 combat Field Pack, which featured a rubberized collar around the mouth, along with more room than the smaller M1956 pack. Inside are a day's rations, a spare set of socks, T-shirt, and a polypropylene sleep shirt. Strapped underneath is a new light weight poncho made of "rip-stop" nylon that was polyurethane coated and printed with the ERDL pattern. This poncho began arriving in Vietnam along with the solid OD green "rip-stop" ponchos in 1968. Secured along with the poncho is a pop-flare. Connected to the left side of the butt pack is a single compass/first aid pouch. Worn on his left hip is a M1956 canteen cover with a plastic 1qt canteen. Suspended from the left side of his H harness is an M-26 grenade. Carried in his hand is an M72 LAW rocket, for use against the numerous NVA bunkers in the Cu Chi area. Around his neck is a St. Christopher medallion.

Close up of $1.00 in M.P.C. Series 651.

Left side of soldier. Note the first aid/compass pouch secured to his buttpack.

Close up of LAW rocket tube. By 1970-71 these would be improved and woul look slightly different.

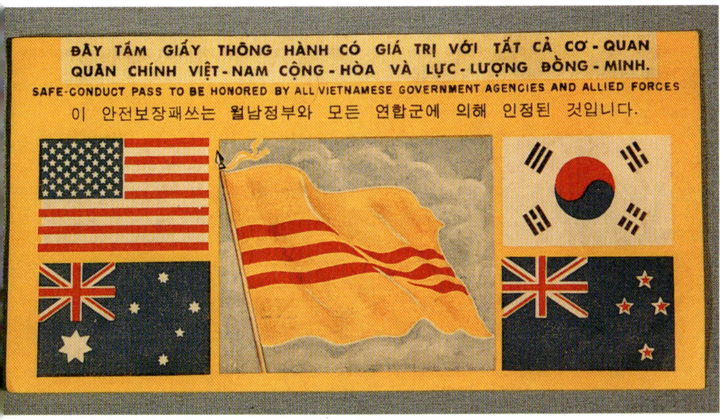

'lose up of safe passage for VC/NVA. These were usually distributed by air in ɔntested areas of South Vietnam.

Close up of reverse side showing a communist soldier arm in arm with an ARVN.

:ompany G, 75th Infantry, "Golf Rangers,"
'eam Alabama, 23d Americal Division
)uang Nam, 1969
ʀTO

"On 01 Feb. '69, the 23rd Infantry Div. (Americal) Comıander, Major General Gettys, activated Company G (Ranger), 5th Infantry."[56] "Equipment and men for this new company were ·btained by deactivating Company E, 51st Infantry. The Rangers engaged in target acquisition, intelligence gathering, and long range surveillance aimed for a twenty-four hour completion period. The staff reasoned that the teams could confirm enemy presence in just 24 hours. Longer missions would have only endangered the teams. The Recon Zone stretched from the Laotian border to the interior mountains, to include scattered regions of Quang Nam, Quang Ngai, and Quang Tin Provinces, nicknamed the 'Suicide Zone.' The Co. referred to themselves as the Americal Rang-

:ompany G, 75th Infantry "Ranger," Team Alabama, 1969.

Co. G Ranger, backside, shows the new Tropical rucksack, along with a LAW anti-tank rocket, and the short whip antenna of his PRC-77 radio. Note the two 2qt canteens with covers secured to the outside of his ruck.

Close up of locally produced Recondo badge for the 23d. The Americal set up its own version of the MACV Recondo school so it could send all of its Ranger and scouts to get additional training, which would give them the edge while on extended patrols.

ers, after the Div. Title, or Golf Rangers G in conformity with the phonetic alphabet. Ranger Teams within the Co. usually took on names of U.S. States, like Hawaii, Ohio, and Texas."[57]

"The 23rd insisted on above average standards for its rangers, including successful completion of the Americals' own Recondo course. The course was typical of the many Div.-level recon schools in country that implemented basic patrolling techniques taught by the Army Ranger school and the MACV Recondo School. Special attention was also given to classroom map reading and radio communications."[58]

This recreation of a RTO with team Alabama is typical of Rangers in late 1969 from the 23rd Americal Div. Uniform consists of ERDL camouflage, which by this time had become standardized for Ranger Companies, as well as most Marine Corps Line Companies. According to Gary Linderer, these were affectionately called "Flower Powers." Face paint was applied by mixing the Arm insect repellent (bug juice) with the two-color Army camo stic which made application to the exposed face, neck, arms, and hanc easier, and last longer. LBE consists of a mixture of M1956 ca vas gear, such as his H-harness paired up with the newer M196 nylon pistol belt with the "Davis" fastener. For carrying the ne 30 round magazine, this Ranger has improvised and turned th nylon 2-quart canteen covers into ammunition pouches. Each 2 quart could accommodate ten 30 round magazines for his CAR 15. Inside his Tropical Rucksack is the team's PRC/77 radio, whic came into service around 1968, and was an improved version c the PRC/25. Many teams opted to carry a second PRC/77 in cas the primary radio became inoperable. Along with the 20 lb. Ra dio, the RTO had to carry extra batteries, spare handsets, and th accessories bag with the additional antennas, and sometimes th security scrambler, which weighed as much as the radio. The RT was also responsible for carrying his own gear as well, such a poncho and liner, weapons cleaning kit, a 5qt collapsible can teen, notebook with plastic cover and pencil (pen would smear extra towel, marker panel, and protective mask. Some team lead ers required each member to carry his own medical kit, individua and in it would be the following: 2 battle dressings, 20 salt tab lets, 24 Tetracycline tablets, 24 Dapsone tablets, 12 cold tablets 12 Polymagma tablets, 8 Chloroquine-Primaquine tablets, 2 Codeine, 6 Dextroamphetamine tablets, and injection kit, Mor phine. Although he carries the teams' radio, mission essential gea was still divided up. The RTO might find himself "humping" th starlight scope, 100 rounds M-60 ammo, five 40mm rounds, claymore mine, 2 trip flares, an AN/GSS-9 anti-intrusion device and at least one LAW rocket. Attached to the outside of his ruc are two of the nylon 2 quart canteen covers that were introduce in late '68, two-quart canteens, 12 foot Swiss seat with D-ring and an M-72 LAW rocket. All of this weight broke the cardina scouting rule of traveling "light and fast." Tropical combat boots or "jungle boots," as they were affectionately known, are the im proved final version that featured a spike resistant insole and th Panama sole pattern tread design.

Close up showing the Tropical Rucksack.

:ompany E, 75th Infantry, "Riverine Rangers," d Brigade, 9th Infantry Division 'an An, 1969 Parakeet Mission"

"Ranger CO.E was formed on 01 February 1969 by inacti- ating Company E, 50th Infantry, and were based at Dong Tam. 'he Rangers were known as the 'Riverine Rangers,' because most f their operations involved canal and river reconnaissance. Al- hough Co. E was only partially assigned to Task Force 117, the Ranger companies' overall wet-patrol tactics, use of naval infil- ration tactics, and operations in inundated areas justified the title RIVERINE' for the entire unit. Co E was made up of eleven 6- nan teams; Ranger teams 11, 13, 14, 15, 16, 17, 19, 21, 22, 24, nd 29. Three of Company E's Teams were kept at Dong Tam, vhile 2 others were stationed with the 1st Brigade at FSB Danger n the Province of Dinh Toung. Task Force 117, 2nd Brigade, Mobile Riverine Force received three Teams dedicated to 'River Raider' patrols, while the three remaining Teams were based at Tan An with the 3rd Brigade for 'Parakeet Flight Duty' and re- on. Parakeet Flights consisted of a full 6 man Team instead of a revious 4 man Team, called Ranger Hunter contingents. The Parakeet helos would fly over waterways as well as land looking or targets. An Airmobile raid was immediately employed once a suitable target was identified as being the enemy. Violent actions once on the ground, as well as a rapid departure, were critical to the success of these raids. The Parakeet missions and tactics re- lied heavily on surprise, as well as rehearsed immediate action drills. The 9th Div. also developed its own Sniper school, and began fitting each team with a qualified sniper. The 9th INF Div. recon units, such as the Riverine and later the 3rd Brigade's 'Go Devil' Rangers waged intelligence gathering operations under circumstances more difficult than those of their parent organiza- tion. Because they worked in the vastly open deltas of S. Viet- nam, and densely populated pro-Viet-Cong areas, the traditional stealth and surprise aspect of maneuverability were lost. The pa- trollers also suffered huge rates of water induced diseases that disabled entire teams."[59]

This recreation Riverine Ranger, CO E, Tan An, 3rd Brigade, is preparing to board one of the choppers for a "Parakeet Flight" mission. On the left sleeve of his ERDL shirt is a U.S. twill 9th INF Div. patch, along with a Vietnamese machine made Co. E Ranger scroll, which lacks the "swallow tail" design. Below that are E-5 chevrons lined with felt that were obtainable at any of the local tailor shops on or off Dong Tam. Underneath his fatigues he wears the "olive green nylon/triacetate sleeping shirt, which is shrink resistant and resembles a pullover sweater. "The knitted

Riverine Ranger, Company E, 3d Brigade 9th Infantry Division, Tan An.

Left side of "Riverine Ranger." Note the two nylon M1967 ammo pouches.

sleep shirt was usually worn at night in a static position and was not intended to be worn if the soldier was on the move or doing strenuous work. It was usually put on after movement or in a defensive position." Worn on his pistol belt are four of the new M1967 nylon ammo pouches. "These are identical to the M-16A1 20 round, small arms case, but in nylon. Grenades could be hung on the outside by the existing side slots and secured by two nylon straps. An additional nylon strap was included inside each pouch, which helped to raise up each magazine to a level at which it could be removed easily."[60] Some soldiers resorted to putting 550-cord or green duct tape at the bottom of the magazine to ease in their removal. Attached to the left side is an SDU-5/E distress marker in its nylon case. Below that is one M-18 smoke grenade. Worn on his right side is a D-ring and an ear plug case painted black. Earplugs were usually worn on the way in or out of patrols while on board the choppers to protect one's hearing. Headgear is an ERDL poplin beret worn over an OD drive on rag. Weapon is the CAR-15.

Close up showing the blackened ear plug case used to hold the small ear plugs

Right side gives a good view of strobe light and additional M1967 ammo pouch.

Close up showing the E Company Ranger scroll, along with the twill 9th Division SSI.

6

1970

5th Battalion, 12th Infantry,
199th Infantry Brigade (Light)
Gia Ray, 1970
Medic

This medical specialist carries the Medical Field Pack, worn correctly as a backpack. The pack was capable of carrying enough bandages for an Infantry Platoon, and sometimes a whole company. Most medics carried triangular bandages, Vaseline gauze, numerous dressings, field dressings, medical cards, antimalarial tablets, water purification tablets, and bacitracin and tetracain ointments, along with numerous cough lozenges and the "cure all' aspirin. A separate outside pocket was intended to hold a wooden splint. There was no SOP for packing the bag; the medic usually filled the pack with what he deemed necessary and what worked. Hanging off each side of the pack, via a D-ring are two

Full figure of medic from the 199th Infantry Brigade.

Left side of medic showing nylon aid bag and twill SSI of the 199th.

Full right side of 199th medic.

Close up showing helmet with personal items in it. Note the "I Support Nixon" button and his nickname "Pig Pen." This is also a good shot of the twill 199th patch.

1qt canteens. Worn across his chest is a locally produced copy of the Unit 1 bag, fabricated out of the nylon lightweight rucksack. Inside would be the surgical kit, blood expander, smaller bandages, dressings, and morphine. Worn on his M1956 pistol belt is a single universal pouch to carry extra 20 round magazines for his M16. Worn on his right hip is a M1911 pistol in a Vietnamese made "cowboy" holster, with an additional pocket for a spare clip. These holsters were fabricated from pigskin or water buffalo, and did not last too long.

Uniform is the final model in cotton "rip-stop" with a single U.S. manufactured twill 199th SSI. M-1 helmet and its reversible camouflage cover would remain unchanged throughout the war. Although an ERDL camouflage cover was in the system in 1969, it would see limited use. "The addition of personnel items, such as the nickname 'Pig-pen,' the metal Christian cross, and the Nixon button were typical of individualization by 1970. Such non-military adornments were tolerated and were an indication of changing times."[61]

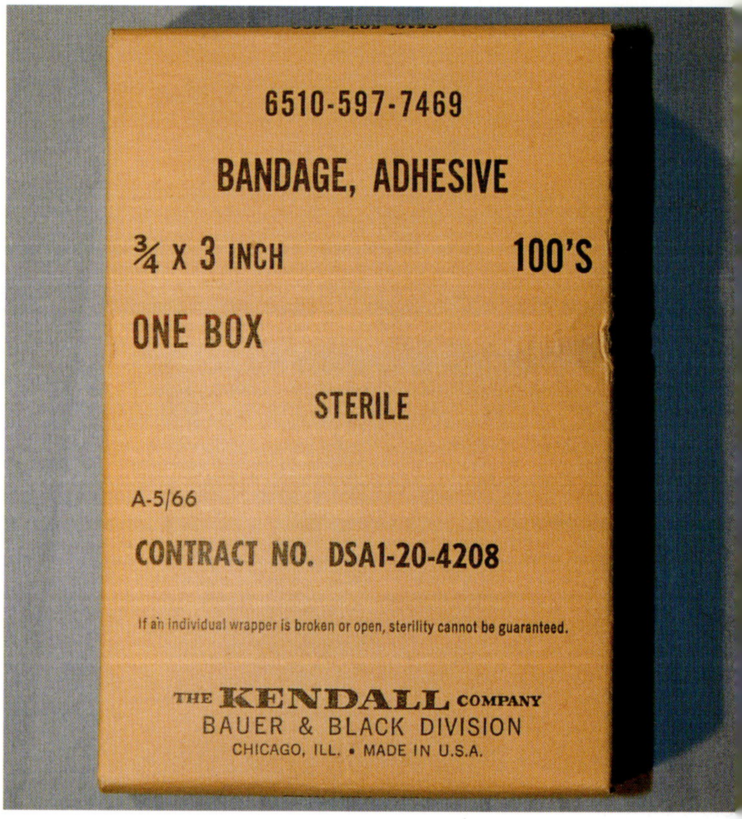

Right: *Close up showing box of 1966 dated Bandages, Adhesive, otherwise known as "Band Aids."*

ull figure back view showing the Medical Field pack.

Close-up of Medical pack, along with the four 1-quart canteens.

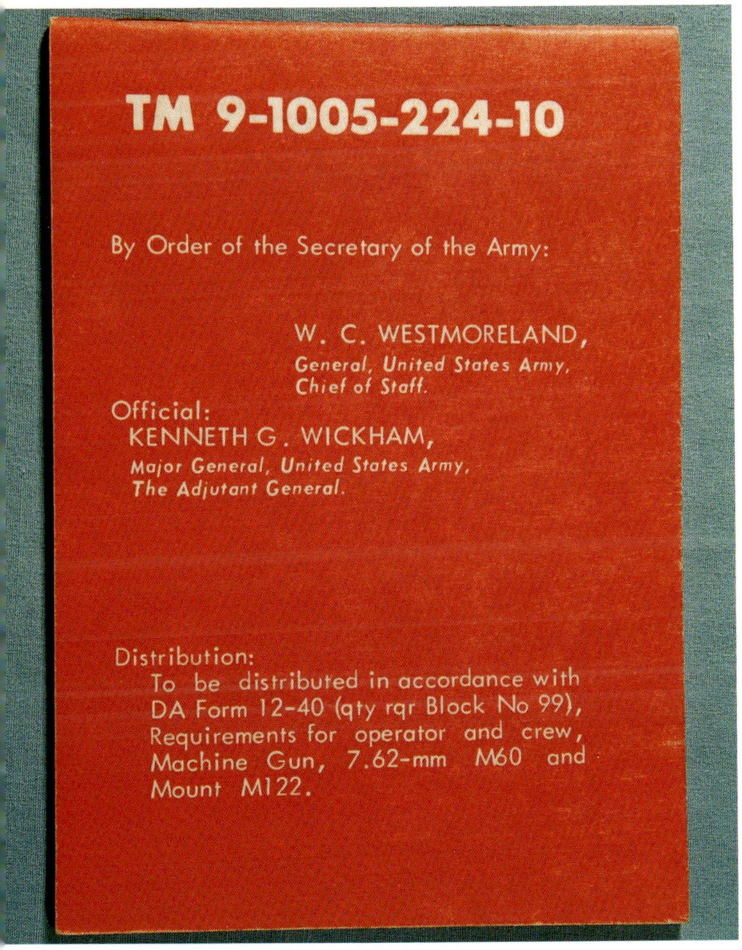

Close up; Rear shot of M60 manual.

Close up of TM on the M60 machine gun. Dated Oct 1970.

Unknown M60 gunner prepares to move out with his Asst. gunner to his right. On his Lightweight rucksack is a 5-quart water bladder, a canvas carrier for the M16 bipod, and extra M60 ammo. Moreover, what appears to be a pneumatic mattress, secured to the bottom of the ruck. Note the tight leg wrappings.

Close up showing black Vietnamese made "cowboy" holster with .45 pistol.

Full figure of Grenadier from the 2nd Bn, 506th Infantry, 101st (AMBL) "Currchee."

Close up showing a bottle of LSA Weapons Oil, Medium.

Grenadier takes a knee during a halt in the action.

Close up showing subdued 101st SSI and banana leaves in the helmet band. Note the M1956 canteen cover is being used to hold numerous 40mm grenades for his M79. Also an item of interest is the subdued 101st patch that has been colored in using the face paint.

Good shot of the rear showing his Tropical ruck, which has been secured to a Lightweight ruck aluminum frame. Note the Post 1969 Claymore bag, which features the hole through the snaps and his machete.

2nd Battalion, 506th Infantry, "Currchee," 101st Division (Airmobile) Infantry FSB Ripcord, Thua Thien Province, 1970 Grenadier

"Fire Support Base 'Ripcord' was built in April 1970 by the 101st about 25 miles west of Hue in Thua Thien Province. It was an essential forward artillery base in the Division summer offensive plans against the A Shau Valley. Like most Firebases, Ripcord was built as part of a network of individually isolated posts garnered mutual protection because they were within artillery range of each other. On march 13th, after delays due to bad weather, Company A of the 2nd Battalion, 506th Infantry air assaulted onto the future 'Ripcord' hill. As soon as the unit landed, it was struck with intense mortar, automatic weapon fire, and recoilless rifle fire. The company evacuated the hill-site two days later. On April 1, after another period of foul weather, Company B of the same unit air-assaulted onto the hill and was greeted by the same hostile reception.

The second Battalion teamed up with the 1st ARVN Regiment to sweep the vicinity around FSB 'Ripcord' for the next week. On April 11, Engineers and the battalion command post were helicoptered in. The Engineers worked unmolested until July 1, when daily mortaring and rocket attacks began to bombard them. The next day, a nearby night defensive position of the battalion was hit hard by elements of the 803d NVA Regiment. Increased barrages and ground movement quickly disclosed North Vietnamese interests in knocking out the base. Fire Support Ripcord became the center of attention in Military Region 1 during the entire month of July."[62]

This grenadier represents one of the paratroopers tasked with patrolling the perimeter of the new Fire Support Base. He wears the final model Jungle Fatigues in rip-stop cotton poplin. Worn on the left sleeve is the SSI of the 101st Airborne. Web gear consists of a pistol belt connected to the M1956 H harness. In the front, the Grenadier has converted two 1qt canteen covers into makeshift ammo pouches for his variety of 40mm M79 shells. Each canteen cover was capable of carrying several H.E. and canister rounds. An additional six rounds are carried in the cotton bandoleer worn across his chest. Two 1qt plastic canteens are carried in the post 1967 canteen cover, which were nothing more

Close up showing canteen covers doubling as ammunition pouches for the M79, along with the cotton bandoleer.

Close up of Vietnamese made "November Ranger" scroll. Company N, 75th Infantry, "Team Julia," 1970.

than an M1956 cover with nylon trim. Additional M79 rounds are carried inside the M18 Claymore bag, which were highly coveted as "carry alls," and could accommodate many more M79 rounds. Note the M18 Claymore bag is the post 1968 variation, which featured the snap with the hole instead of the solid snap. Rucksack is the Tropical ruck mounted to the lightweight frame. An M1942 machete in its M1967 sheath is secured to the top of the ruck.

M1 helmet is worn with the "Mitchell" pattern cover and the Camouflage Helmet Band, to which he has secured numerous banana leaves and a 101st SSI, which he has attempted to subdue with the green face paint.

Full figure of Company N, 75th Infantry, Ranger, 173d Airborne Infantry Brigade.

Company N, 75 Infantry (Rangers),
173d Airborne Brigade
Operation "Washington Green," 1970
Ranger

"Company N was activated on 1 Feb '69 by transforming the 74th Infantry Detachment into a Ranger Company tailored for brigade reconnaissance support and known as 'NOVEMBER' Rangers. The Company became operational on 9 Feb 1969, and

Close up showing the Ranger's fighting load complete with M-26 grenades. Additional grenades are carried in his M-16 pouches.

Full figure of Ranger with bi-pod legs up.

Full figure of Team Julia member, 1970.

its twelve teams were immediately deployed to forestall the projected enemy Tet-69 offensive in Binh Dinh Province. General Barnes anticipated that Ranger patrol saturation would screen enemy buildups and allow him to counter NVA/VC movements with regular brigade forces. The Company's twelve ranger teams, labeled by international phonetic letter codes, such as team Alpha, were instructed to use artillery and aerial firepower against enemy targets and were infiltrated into the An Lao, An Lo, Suoi Ca, and 506 valleys; the Highland Fishhook; the Crows foot; and the Nui Ba and Tiger mountains."[63]

This recreated November Ranger, Team Juliet, Binh Province, is typical of Rangers participating in Operation "WASHINGTON GREEN" Nov 1969 to Dec 1970. Headgear worn here is the popular OD cotton boonie hat that has been modified to a short brim variation by cutting off about an inch of the brim. Weapon is a captured RPD (Rapid People Destroyer) in 7.62-

Right: *Sgt. Ronald G. Baker H-Co. 75th Inf. (RANGER) 1st Air Cav. Division 1970. Sgt. Baker stands outside of his hooch wearing a fully badged uniform, along with the black beret. The beret features a large "beer can" 75th If DI Crest, about the size of a U.S. half dollar. All the members of Co. H wore this crest or a handsewn variation. All 118 men of H Co wore the OG 107 jungle fatigues fully badged around the company area instead of the ERDL camouflage uniforms so often associated with the Rangers. This is evident from Sgt. Baker's Ranger yearbook and photo albums, which show the Rangers only wearing the ERDL on missions. Circa 1970. (John Jones collection.)*

Close up showing the rear of the Ranger. Note the 2qt canteen and cover on his pistol belt and the additional 2qt canteen secured to his Tropical rucksack by a D-ring. Also note this Ranger has turned his M1956 canteen cover into a makeshift ammo pouch for a belt of ammo for his RPD.

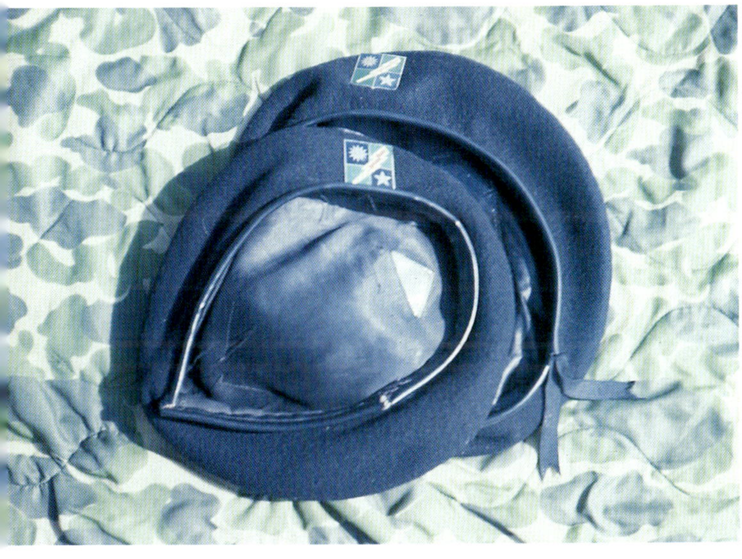

Close up showing two black Ranger berets that feature a tin 75th Infantry badge. These both once belonged to Sgt. Baker, Co H Rangers, 1st Cavalry Division. (Courtesy Bob Norris)

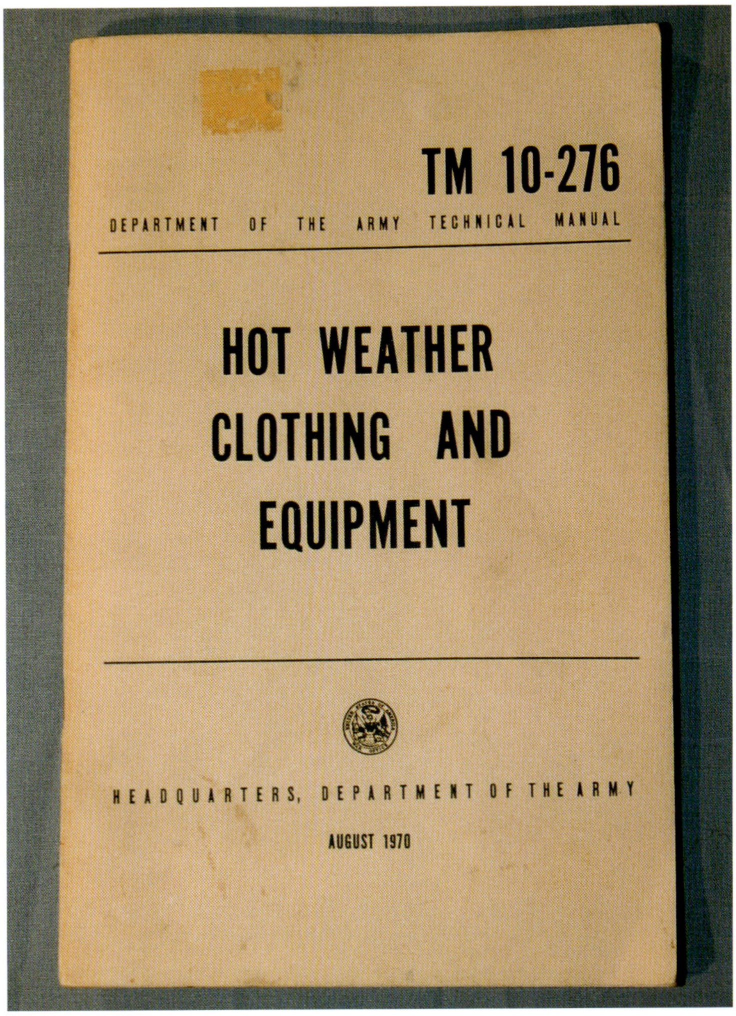

Close up of TM 10-276; Hot Weather Clothing and Equipment. Inside is a description of all the new MLCE, camouflage, hammocks, and jungle boots.

mm. The Ruchnoi Pulemet Degtyarev (RPD) was adopted in 1948 as the standard squad automatic weapon of the Soviet Army. It is chambered for the Model 43 intermediate-size cartridge, as are the assault rifle (AK) and carbine (SKS). The barrel is chrome plated and is not of the quick change type, and is one of the lightest belt fed machine guns in use at this time (1970). The RPD was made lighter by cutting the barrel at the gas tube, thus losing the front site and bipod legs and cutting off a portion of the buttstock. Some LRRP and Ranger teams preferred that no one carried foreign weapons like the RPD or AK. Many times, you could not see the enemy, only hear him, and many teams fired by sound alone, occasionally resulting in friendly fire incidents for team members with foreign weapons. Over his shoulder he carries a claymore bag with two additional 100 round drums for his RPD. On his back he carries the new "Tropical rucksack," or "jungle ruck," which came in Olive Green, Army shade 106, mildew and water resistant nylon. The ruck offered a large central pocket, three smaller outer pockets, and a Velcro closed pocket underneath the main flap. Much like the ARVN Ranger pack, the Tropical ruck featured its own integrated spring steel X-frame, with a rivet placed uncomfortably in the center. Many soldiers took the X-frame completely out or bent it inwards to avoid the rivet, which was strategically placed at the center of the wearer's back. The ruck also featured a quick release buckle on either shoulder strap to allow it to be jettisoned during emergencies. Inside his ruck he

Unidentified Co H Ranger inside of hooch. Circa 1970. (John Jones collection.)

Sgt. Baker outside of Co H's Ranger Lounge. He wears cut-off tigerstripe fatigues and sandals. Note the Schlitz's beer logo on the door and the Ranger crest above the door to the Ranger lounge. 1970. (Jon Jones collection.)

Sgt. Baker in civilian running shoes and socks in company area. Note the tiger-stripe shorts. (Jon Jones Collection)

Sgt. Baker in cut-off T-shirt and hippie sandals. (Jon Jones Collection)

Unidentified Co. H Ranger in hooch wearing tour jacket. (Jon Jones Collection)

carries an additional 500 rounds of ammunition, bringing his grand total to 800 rounds of 7.62mm. An M-17 mask, a block of C-4, one radio battery, 5 LRP rations, an AN/PVS-2 night scope, 1 claymore mine, a poncho and poncho-liner, one marker panel, his personal first-aid kit, and a 2-qt. Canteen are also in his ruck. Attached to the outside of his ruck are a 5-quart water bladder (top) and two 1-quart canteens on either side.

"The Rangers maximized team potential with new equipment. For example, Company N received an experimental system that upgraded their ability to fire electronically detonated Claymore mines—the staple of ranger ambushes in Vietnam—through the use of Remote Firing Devices. These devices (boxes) were pre-positioned and concealed along ambush zones and linked into multiple Claymore mines that could be fired by rangers with hand held firing devices from distances up to a thousand yards away. The rangers improved this system by using Personal Seismic Detectors in conjunction with the Remote Firing Devices. Another refinement was the use of concussion grenades in the center of remotely triggered ambush zones so that a few stunned enemy soldiers were left alive for capture."[64] "During this period of operation WASHINGTON GREEN, the Brigade was commanded in turn by Brig. Gen Hubert Cunningham, who took over in August 1969, and Brig. Gen Ray Ochs from August 1970 forward. Both Generals were staunch believers in 'Airborne' esprit and believed that special ranger privileges might undermine paratrooper camaraderie. For these reasons the black ranger berets were banned, despite their common use by other ranger outfits."[65]

1st Brigade, 3d Battalion, 327th Infantry; "Hawk Recon," 101st (Airmobile) Division
Phu Bai, 1970
Recondo

"One imaginative 1st Brigade Initiative was the employment of its 3 Inf. Batt. Reconnaissance Platoons as Recondo. Each 20 man plus platoon was initially equipped for more conventional operations, but the nature of the war and II CTZ's terrain prevented effective use of their mobility. The platoons turned in their jeeps and trained extensively in ambush and reconnaissance pa-

Full figure shot of 327th "Hawk Recon" soldier, 101st Airborne Division, 1970.

Close up showing the binoculars with the case.

Close up upper torso of Hawk Reconner. Note the 30 round magazine in his M16 rifle.

Close up right side of "Hawk Recon" soldier. Note the post 1969 M18 Claymor bag with the holes in the snaps.

trols using Recondo techniques. They were to patrol assigned areas, and once the enemy was found, Airmobile reaction forces, supported by artillery and gunship, would respond. Each of the three platoons also adopted a fitting title: 3-327 Infantry "Hawk Recon"; 2-502 "Recondos"; and 1-327 Infantry "Tiger Force."[66]

This re-creation wears the ever popular bush hat, or "boonie hat." This variation in the ERDL pattern was relatively common among elitists and Marine Corps Units by 1969. Web gear is again a mixture of cotton and nylon gear; the new MLCE nylon H-harness is worn in conjunction with the 50/50 cotton/nylon pistol belt, along with two M-16 ammo pouches designed to hold 4 M-16 20 round magazines. Attached to (his) left side, in its own nylon pouch is the SDU-5/E distress marker, along with a flash guard. Worn on both the left and right sides are the M-18 smoke grenades, RED. Worn around his neck is the OD green triangular bandage, or drive on rag, that could be used to wipe the sweat from his face.

On the left sleeve of his green dominant ERDL pattern shir is a Vietnamese procured SSI of the 101st Airborne Div., alon with a Vietnamese made scroll of the 2nd Batt., 327 INF "HAWK RECON." Above his left pocket, obscured by his gear is a Vietnamese made U.S. ARMY strip and airborne qualification badge which is also in country made. The Lightweight rucksack, firs issued to Special Forces in 1963 as the T62-1, was standardize by 1965, replacing the small butt pack. The ruck featured a large nylon water-resistant bag, with three smaller external pockets large enough to accommodate one 1-quart canteen each. The nylon ruck came with its own tubular aluminum frame, with the bag affixe to top or bottom depending on the preference of the soldier. Attached to the outside via the double eyelet web tabs is the newe XM28 Lightweight Protective mask in its nylon case. Anothe feature was the quick release device located on the shoulder strap which allowed the wearer to easily discard the ruck. Altogether the ruck and frame weighed only 3 pounds, empty.

'lose up of the left side of Reconner. Note the Hawk Recon scroll and Vietnamese nade 101st Airborne badge. This is also a good shot of the XM28.

Full figure of M79 Grenadier from the 6th Bn, 31st Infantry, 9th Infantry Division, 1970.

th Battalion, 31st Infantry (Polar Bears),
d Brigade (Separate) 9th Infantry Division
'an Giuoc, 1970
Grenadier

"The 3d Brigade (Separate) of the 9th Infantry Div. Served inder the command of the 25th Infantry Div. Performing operaions in the southern III Corps. Tactical Zone from July 1969 unil its departure from Vietnam. Its base camp of Tan An wasloated in the extreme southern portion of the III Corps. The major ortion of the 9th Inf. Div. Departed Vietnam in Sept. 1969, leavng the 3d Brigade (GO DEVILS) the sole remaining element of he division in Vietnam from that time forward."[67]

Ammunition for the M-79 grenade launcher was issued and isually carried in six round cotton bandoleers, which consisted of two, 3 round pockets and a strap. Each pocket contained a plastic "egg crate" style three round holder to keep the grenades n place. These cotton bandoleers were unsatisfactory because he straps often snagged on vines and vegetation, causing the rounds to fall out of the carrier. In 1965, a Special Forces NCO showed his makeshift grenade vest to a Natick Laboratories representative. His vest was copied, and in 1966 the first nylon versions were airlifted to Vietnam. These vests were bright green nylon, similar to the vests given to members of the flight deck crews aboard U.S. Navy Aircraft Carriers. "The vest featured four

Close up of Third Brigade Yearbook.

Full figure showing the left side of Grenadier. Note the U.S. twill 9th Infantry Division SSI

Full figure of the back of the Grenadier. Note the "chow sock" hanging fron his nylon grenade vest.

Close up of helmet showing dry socks and bug juice.

pockets in the front, each holding three rounds apiece, and wer secured with a nylon strip with Velcro. The vest was closed ir front with a zipper. The vests were well received, but becaus they were made out of nylon, they were hot and uncomfortable In 1967, a modified vest was produced, replacing the body of th vest with nylon netting. The vest could be adjusted by three elas tic cross straps down the center of the back, and by drawstring along each side below the armholes. The front closed with a Velcrc tape fastener. The new improved vest contained six sets of thre grenade pockets, four in the front and two in the rear. This pro duced a 18 round carrying capacity. These vests also incorpo rated the M1967 plastic snaps. These vests began arriving in Viet nam in early 1967. By 1969, a new and improved vest was intro duced in 1969 and could accommodate 24 rounds in the thre rows of grenade pockets on each side in the front. The hard tc reach pockets at the rear of the vest were eliminated, and the plastic snaps were changed to metal ones. Worn here by this grenadier is the final version, which would continue on in service for anothe 30 years."[68]

Web gear consists of a 1966 horizontal weave pistol belt witl a single M26 hand-grenade. On the right side is the twin cel magazine pouch for his M1911 45. cal. pistol. Next to it is the M1911 pistol in the black M1916 leather holster. On his left side is the M1942 machete in the M1967 sheath. Behind it are twc

Close up showing Zippo lighter and Marlboro cigarettes. Note the U.S. produced 9th Inf. SSI and the two large pockets on the grenade vest. These were provided for the large White Parachute Flares and Star Cluster rounds.

Upper torso showing the vest. Note the 2qt canteen secured by a D-ring to his vest.

canvas canteen covers which hold two 1qt plastic canteens. D-ringed to his Grenade vest is a polypropylene 2qt canteen. Attached to the back yoke of his vest is a single OD green boot-sock full of C-rations, otherwise called a "chow sock."

Note the numerous items attached in this grenadier's helmet band, synonymous with members of the 9th Infantry Division, who were constantly subjected to wet, swampy operational areas. Weapon is the M79 grenade launcher.

Taplin Boots, sometimes known as the "Delta Boot."

Close up showing the universal pouch with a compass/first aid pouch, the M1942 machete in the M1967 sheath, and the "chow sock" tied to the back of the vest.

Full figure showing the Grenadier in action firing his M79.

Full figure of Company F, Ranger, 25th Infantry Division. 1970.

Company F, 75 Infantry, "Tropical Rangers," Team 38, Recon Strike Force 3d Brigade, 25th Division Ap Ben Dinh, 1970 RTO

"These Ranger were known as either 'Fox Rangers' or the 'Tropical Rangers,' from the 25th Inf. Div. nickname. Tropic Lighting Ranger teams reached obj. areas by foot patrol, helicopter airlifts, naval boat insertion, or APC. A common ranger mode of entry into populated areas involved blending with a larger force, then remaining behind in hidden positions. The Ranger Co. provided each Brigade with teams to collect Intel., and if the opportunity arose, to inflict casualties on the enemy. Each of the three field platoons initially contained three or four 8-man teams. Ranger teams 11-14 supported the 1st Brigade, covering Tay Ninh Province. Teams 21-23 supported the 2nd Brigade in Hau Nghia Province, and teams 31-33 assisted the 3rd Brigade, also in Hau Nghia Province. At least one sniper-qualified individual was assigned to each team. Ranger operating methods were redirected toward ambush and combat reconnaissance exploitation. Air rescue missions were performed with sniper teams."[69] "From Nov. 1969 to the end of April 1970, most of the Tropical Ranger Teams were employed in direct support of the 3rd Brigade. These combat reconnaissance efforts were directed against the enemy An Ninh

Close up showing the two universal pouches, 3 cotton bandoleers, lensetic compass, and the old style square microphone handset for the PRC 25 radio.

Full shot of the Ranger utilizing the PRC-77 Radio.

Full figure of Company F. 75th Infantry, "Ranger," 25th Infantry Division. Note the numerous cotton bandoleers with M16 magazines.

Full figure shot of the Ranger showing the PRC77 Radio.

infiltration corridor. The rangers performed about 90 patrols a month, and worked target sectors at Nui Ba Den, north of Cu Chi, outside Tri Tam, and within both the Straight Edge woods and Renegade woods. The most serious ranger incident during the An Nihn corridor reconnaissance occurred in response to Division Intel. assessments sent to 3d Brigade at the end of March. The Intel. Summaries indicated that sizeable VC elements were slipping back into the Renegade Woods. The woods constituted a well-known VC refitting area and were covered by vine choked double canopy jungle. Helicopter insertions were difficult due to the few open fields, which consisted of high elephant grass divided by hedgerows and contained either brush or deadwood. On the morning of 2 April 1970 the 3d Brigade commander, Col. Smith, directed Capt. S Chierholz to send two ranger teams into the Renegade woods and scout out the situation. Within an hour, a thirteen-man recon strike force, composed of teams 38 and 39, was assembled for the mission. The rangers were airlifted into the region by helicopters, dropped into the landing zone near the South Van Co Dong river, and proceeded toward the tree line and the direction of the ruined village of Ap Ben Dinh. The ranger column was raked by machine gun fire, and had run smack into entrenched elements of the 27 1st VC Regiment. Outnumbered and outflanked, the encircled rangers fought off numerous attacks before a single UH-1H Helicopter, flown by WO1 Tonelli and Capt. Tocco, flew in under withering machinegun fire and pulled the team out of danger."[70]

Rangers in the 25th, such as this RTO, were issued and/or allowed to purchase the ERDL camouflage uniform for ranger missions. The four-color camouflage uniform is seen here in the "Green Dominant" pattern produced in 1968 in the "rip-stop" cotton poplin. Web gear consists of the new M1967 (MLCE) Modernized Load Carrying Equipment suspender, which like the cotton H-harness connected to the pistol belt in four places, but with the new fasteners at the ends. An additional set of 'clamp fasteners' was added on the shoulder for securing the new M1967 nylon butt pack as a light marching pack. A 1966 style pistol belt with the horizontal weave is seen connected to his new H-harness. On it are two universal pouches, each with a single M26 grenade in the slot, secured with the strap. On each side is worn a single canteen cover with 1qt canteen. Around his waist is the M17 Protective mask in its carrier. Across his chest are three cotton bandoleers, each with seven 20 round M16 magazines. Se-

Close up showing back of AN/PRC 77 Radio. Note the two red M18 smoke are placed higher than the one condensed smoke.

Side view, showing Spare Parts Bag, which has been modified, M17 mask i case, and the new 1967 era canteen cover with the nylon trim.

Upper torso shot showing the Ranger's fighting load.

cured to one of the cotton bandoleers is a compass/first aid pouch On his left side he carries a single M18 smoke grenade. The AN PRC 77 Radio, seen here, is carried on the canvas carrying harness, which could be connected and worn in lieu of an H-harness

Headgear is the ERDL pattern boonie hat, produced in 196 in "rip-stop" cotton poplin. Rangers were issued these as well a OD boonie hats, or could easily purchase them or any other typ of "boonie" hat at one of the numerous tailor shops.

Full figure of 2nd Bn. 8th Infantry, 1st Cavalry Division, Cambodia 1970.

Full figure showing RTO utilizing the PRC77.

2nd Battalion, 8th Cavalry,
1st Cavalry Division, Task Force Shoemaker
Operation "Toan Thang" (Total Victory) #43
Cambodia, 1970
Radioman

"At daybreak on May 1, 1970, heavy artillery boomed across the Cambodian border as the last bomb from six B-52 bombing runs crashed into the earth. Then, the tanks and armored personnel carriers of Maj. Gen. Elvy B. Roberts' 1st Cavalry Division (Airmobilc) clanked onto Cambodian soil. Task Force Shoemaker's Operation Toan Thang #43 had as its objective nothing less than the field command HQ for all communist activities in South Vietnam. Major General Roberts' 1st Cav. had reinforced its commitment to the operation with another brigade, and had

Close up showing the RTO's helmet and a single bottle of bug juice.

Close up showing the RTO's rucksack. Note the twill 1st Cavalry SSI and his SPC 4 rank.

Full figure shot of the rear of the RTO.

Upper torso of 1st Cav. RTO. Note the lack of LBE, he only wears a cotton bandoleer to hold magazines for his M16.

thirteen tank and infantry battalions rolling across Cambodia within a week. The initial impression that Operation TOAN THANG #43 would bring the NVA into the open battle soon gave way to the realization that the North Vietnamese were evading. The expectation of crushing battlefield victories vaporized as the long awaited Cambodian incursion became a matter of seizing and destroying massive abandoned supply dumps. One depot complex contained so many military stores and foodstuffs that it was dubbed 'The City.' On May 6, the 1st Cav leaped into Cambodia on its second thrust by air-assaulting two battalions northeast of Bu Op. During this operation a second huge depot was uncovered, and engineers had to build an overland road so the materials could be hauled out."[71] "All Americans were out of Cambodia by June 29, 1970, although several South Vietnamese operations continued. The operation had been militarily successful despite the fact that the NVA/VC main force units simply eluded the advancing allies. The Cambodian campaign gave the American Army a welcome relief from routine operations and put a capstone on the service of several units scheduled for pending departure from Vietnam."[72]

This 1st Cav Trooper is typical of the men involved in the push into Cambodia on May 1, 1970, to destroy the NVA/VC sanctuaries. Uniform is the final pattern in Rip-stop with twill SSI sub 1st Cav. Patch, Vietnamese produced SPC 4 rank, along

Photo showing RTO kneeling utilizing the radio.

Close up showing the RTO's Lightweight rucksack and his PRC77 Radio.

Full figure showing Company E, 75th Infantry, "Ranger" 3d Brigade 9th Infantry Division. (Separate) 1970.

with cotton U.S. Army strip. An OD green drive on rag is worn around his neck to prevent chaffing.

Note the lack of LBE; instead, this trooper wears a single bandoleer around his waist to carry the numerous 20 round magazines for his M-16 rifle.

The RTO carries his PRC/77 with the short tape antenna attached to his lightweight rucksack frame, with the nylon bag over it. Connected to the outside of the Lightweight ruck are the radio accessory bag, 2 1qt canteens and covers, an M18 smoke grenade, and a compass/first aid pouch. In his helmet band is secured a bottle of insect repellent, or "bug juice." Weapon is the M-16A1 rifle.

3d Brigade, Company E (Ranger) 75th Infantry, 9th Infantry Division, Go Devils
Long An Province, 1970
Grenadier

"During May and June of 1970, elements of the 3d Brigade, 9th Div. invaded the Parrots Beak area of Cambodia. The Go-Devil Rangers were left behind to monitor Long An Province as an 'economy of force' precaution. The rangers covered the brigade's Vietnam operational area by staging a number of small roving ambushes, supplemented by 'aquabush' expeditions using Kenner boats. During the same period, the brigade fought without the benefit of its ranger assets during the battle of Cambodia.

Close up showing the Chi-Com style canteen cover, along with the M18 Claymore bag, which could hold quite a few 40mm rounds.

Ranger from the 3d Brigade, 9th Infantry Division, 1970.

Close up showing the pre-69 M18 Claymore bag with the solid snaps. This is a good view of the Chi-Com style canteen cover on the vest.

Close up showing the grenadier removing a 40mm round from one of the 12 pockets.

Close up showing the front pockets of the ammo vest.

Close up of the Ranger's Jungle boots.

Shoe, Comfort, Man's Low Blucher, otherwise known as the "Bivouac Slipper."

During June, the rangers developed the tactic of vectoring patrols in reaction to ground radar sighting."[73]

Photos in the Third Brigade yearbook show the Go-Devil Rangers being delivered to their AO in both the Kenner boats and the PACVs. It also shows them wearing very little gear and equipment, which would most likely mean a short patrol.

This Go-Devil Ranger, obviously on a short patrol, wears a pair of ERDL cotton poplin trousers that he has turned into shorts, for all the inundated muddy areas he has to patrol through. A makeshift grenade vest, that has been fabricated from a ERDL coat, is worn over an additional ERDL shirt. The vest has 12 pockets, each secured with a Vietnamese made button, and capable of holding a single 40mm grenade for the M79 grenade launcher. On each hip is a crude Chi-Com style canteen holder built into the vest in the same ERDL material, also secured with a button. On each breast is a single patch pocket, for smaller items. Across the back is a large pocket, also secured with Vietnamese made buttons. The vest is closed in front by means of a zipper. Although the nylon, M79 ammo vest were standardized by 1970, it was not uncommon to see soldiers, especially Rangers or line Infantry, wearing "make-shift" ammo vests like these, or ones to hold twenty round magazines for the M-16 rifle. Additional M79 rounds are carried in his M18 Claymore bag, which is worn slung across his chest.

Headgear is a Vietnamese made black wool beret, usually reserved for wear in the rear with some type of 75th Infantry device affixed to it; this Ranger has chosen to wear it on operations instead. Worn around his neck is the ever-popular OD green triangular bandage. Jungle boots featuring the Vibram sole are present in 1970, although many preferred the Panama soles.

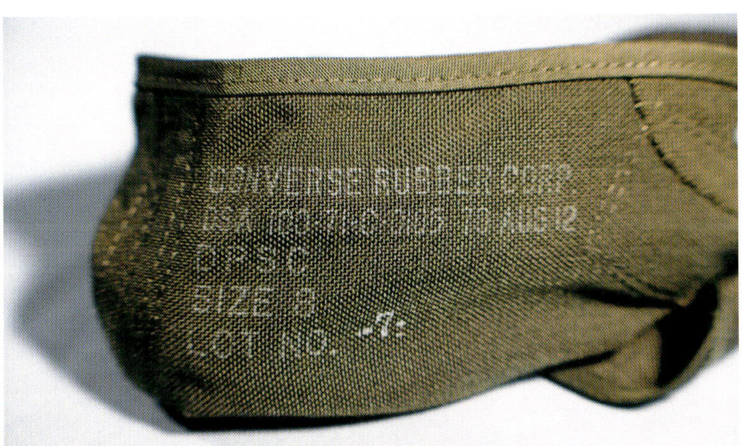

Close up showing the printed label inside the slipper.

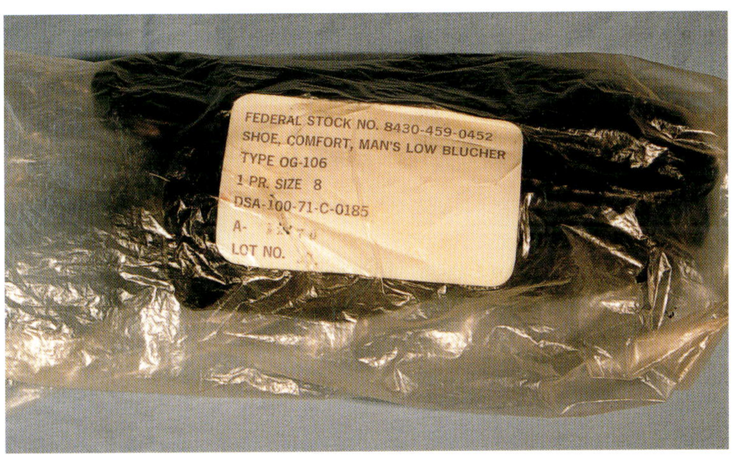

Close up showing the slippers as they were issued inside the bag with the Federal Stock Number.

7

1971

3d Battalion, 187th Infantry (Airmobile Infantry)
"Rakkasans,"
101st Airmobile Infantry Division
Phu Bai, 1971
Platoon Leader

This Rakkasan Platoon Leader wears the M1965 Field Jacket for the cold monsoons of the Phu Bai area. "The 9 ounce cotton sateen jacket, OG Army shade 207, was standardized on 29 Sept. 1966. The jacket featured rounded collars, snap pockets closures, and Velcro sleeve closures. The new coat lacked the trim appearance of the M1951 coat, but was more durable and had a detachable hood that could be zippered into the collar."[74] Worn on the Shoulder Tabs are the First Lieutenant's Rank, sewn on. Worn above the two upper pockets is a U.S. Army strip, nametape, and basic Airborne wings. Under the garment is worn the Field Jacket liner, which is made out of the same material as the wet weather

Platoon leader from the 3dBattalion, 187th Infantry, "Rakkasans" 101st Airborne Division, 1971.

Full figure showing the Platoon leader. Note the WWII shotgun and modified nylon M1967 ammo pouches.

Rear View of "Rakkasan" shows the 2qt canteen and cover. Note the XM28 mask in its case is barley visible.

Platoon leader with M1 helmet off. Note the gray civilian sweatshirt worn underneath his M1965 Field jacket.

poncho liner. Along with that is worn a civilian gray cotton sweatshirt, probably sent over from the states.

Minimal LBE is worn, due to the duration of the patrol. Modified M1967 nylon ammo pouches are worn in front, having the plastic squeeze catch fasteners replaced with two metal snaps, in order to hold shotgun rounds instead of four 20 round magazines. Worn on the left side is a cover canteen with the newer post 1967 nylon trim containing a single 1qt canteen. On the right side is a nylon carrier for the improved XM28 Light Weight Protective Mask. Worn in the middle of the back is the 2qt collapsible canteen with nylon cover, which would remain unchanged for the rest of the war. Secured by a D-ring from his H-harness is an additional 1qt canteen. Carried in the pockets of his "rip-stop" trousers are additional boxes of shotgun rounds for his WWII Stevens shotgun. Headgear is the M1 steel pot with a slightly torn "Mitchell pattern" camouflage cover. Jungle boots with the improved Panama soles are worn with a pair of civilian purchased white tube socks.

Full figure 60 gunner, 1971.

Full rear shot of the 60 gunner. Note his Tropical ruck is mounted to the Lightweight frame.

3d Battalion, 22nd Infantry,
2d Brigade, 25th Infantry Division
Xuan Loc, 1971
Machine Gunner

"The 3d Battalion, 22d Infantry was part of the 4th Infantry Division until officially transferred to the 25th Infantry Division on 1 August 1967, where it stayed until its departure on 20 April 1971."[75] "The main scope of ground activities for U.S. units was concentrated in patrolling and sweeping the rocket belts of various critical installations. Rocket belts were strips of land from which the NVA/VC could launch barrages into the cities. This security role was dubbed "dynamic defense" by the Army, and by the end of the year all U.S. formations had been phased into this new mission near critical installation complexes."[76]

This 60 gunner, or "Pig man" (as they were sometimes called, because they "humped" the "Pig," a nickname for the M60 machine gun), wears the final model U.S. jungle fatigues in "rip-stop" cotton poplin, devoid of all patches. Note the complete lack of web gear, indicating a short patrol. The machine gunner has draped a 150 round belt of 7.62 ammo across his chest, and has additional ammo inside his Tropical rucksack. Note how the gunner has used the OD green towel as a pad to cushion the weight of the M60 machine gun. The gun is being carried in the only comfortable position that many commanders and NCO alike frowned on, because the gun was not at the "ready." However, notice there is no sling for the gun, so this is the only way the gunner has to carry it. Seen here is another example of the Tropical rucksack being connected to the Lightweight ruck frame. Although the Tropical ruck came with a frame, it was uncomfortable and put the ruck right up against the wearer's back, preventing air flow, and many times caused "prickly heat." Another shortcoming of the Tropical ruck was the rivet placed in the center of the steel X frame. This was placed right at the center of the wearer's back, and was extremely uncomfortable when the ruck was fully loaded. With the Tropical mounted to the Lightweight aluminum frame, the wearer had the best of both worlds, a large pack capable of carrying many items, and a comfortable frame that rode on your hips and helped distribute the weight evenly and kept your back

Close up of Tropical with 2qt canteen secured with a D ring.

Close up showing the head and shoulders of a very tired "Pig Man."

from becoming soaked with sweat. Inside his ruck is the new waterproof, lightweight poncho, with hood, which is made of coated nylon, and the nylon poncho liner. Secured inside is the M1942 machete with the olive green plastic sheath, or "self-sharpening sheath," which featured a built-in tungsten carbide blade sharpener, M1967. Connected to the top of the ruck frame is a 2-quart canteen, which was made of an ethylene-vinyl acetate and had a twist off cap that is identical to that of the 1-quart canteen. Connected to the outside of his ruck is a single 1qt canteen in the M1956 canvas cover.

Close up showing the M60 being carried over the shoulder. Note the OD green towel is being used as a cushion.

Full figure of Company L, 75th Infantry Ranger, 101st Airborne, 1971.

Company L 75th (Infantry) "Ranger,"
101st Airborne Division
Team Julia
Rao Trang River Valley, 1971
Team Leader

"On 02 Sept. 1971, Ranger team Julia was inserted by helicopter in the mountainous triple canopy jungle near the Rao Trang river. The five-man patrol spotted a well-camouflaged trail cut with machetes about a week before and followed it past an abandoned enemy sleeping area. The trail crossed several rocky, leech filled streams. The team attempted to transmit by voice on radio and failed, because loud Vietnamese music and song recordings jammed all FM frequencies. Throughout the patrol, whenever the team attempted to transmit using voice mode, the enemy jammed their radio frequencies with blaring music. On the second day, the rangers investigated another hidden trail thick in the jungle shrubbery that was interspersed with bamboo thickets and banana palms. The team then set up overnight positions. On the fourth day, the patrollers found a third hardpacked trail last traveled within the week. While investigating the trail the Rangers

Close up showing ruck with a single 1qt canteen and cover, M18 Claymore bag and 2qt canteen and cover.

Full figure showing the left side of the Ranger. Note the addition of an M79 for added firepower.

Full figure showing the right side of the Ranger. Note the 30 round magazine in his M16A1 rifle. Most Rangers in Co. L had access to the newer CAR-15, but this one has chosen the M16A1 instead.

Full figure shot of the rear of the Ranger showing his heavy ruck.

Close up showing the 101st SSI with a Vietnamese made Airborne Arc and U.S. made E-5 rank.

Close up showing the left side of the Ranger.

Close up showing the 5qt water bladder on the rucksack.

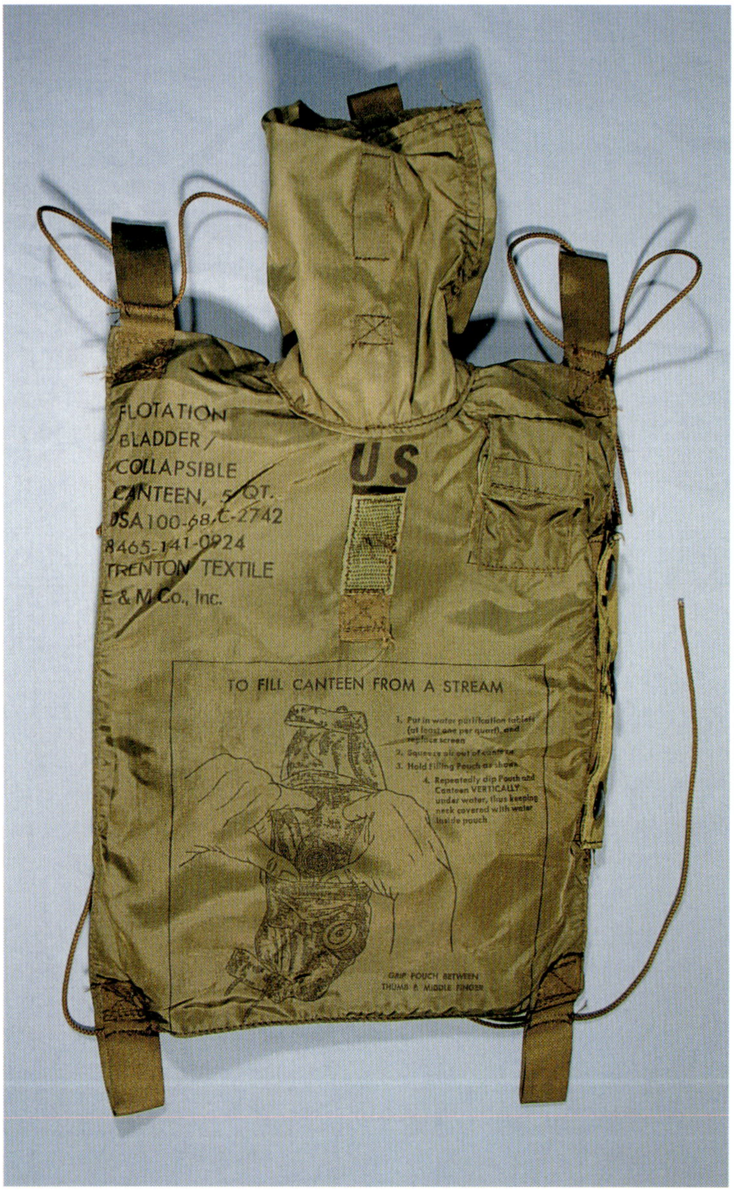

Close up showing the Flotation Bladder, Collapsible Canteen, 5 QT. DSA 100-68-C-2742.

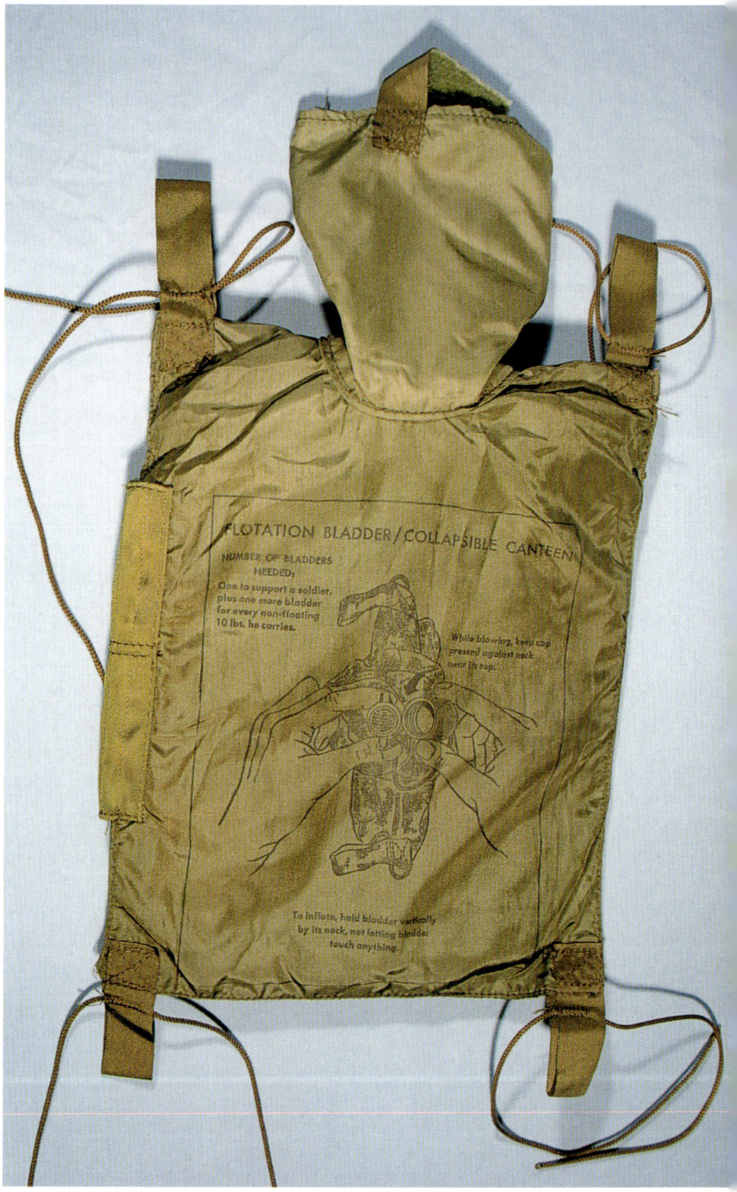

Close up of reverse side of 5QT Bladder and instruction label.

found a discarded North Vietnamese poncho and tree branches marked by carved arrows underneath X-slashes. The Rangers spent the remainder of the day cutting a clearing. Later that afternoon, helicopters arrived over a pre-planned site and hoisted the team out using ropes. The five-day expedition of Team Julia provided valuable information on previous unknown enemy traffic routes and exemplified Ranger reconnaissance missions."[77]

This team Julia member wears a set of green dominant ERDL pattern camouflage, sometimes referred to as "Flower-Powers." By this time, all Ranger Co. and select line Infantry units were receiving these camouflage uniforms. On his left sleeve is an SSI of the 101st with a Vietnamese made AIRBORNE arc. Below and on the opposite sleeve are E-5 stripes.

Web gear consists of an M1967 nylon pistol belt with the Davis quick release buckle. Worn on the left side is an M1956 canvas canteen cover with four 20 round magazines. Next to that is a new M16A1 Small Arms Pouch, containing four more 20

Close up showing the Ranger's mid section and his fighting load. Note the canteen cover is used to hold 20 round magazines for his M16A1.

Close up of ruck and the early model M18 Claymore bag with the solid snaps.

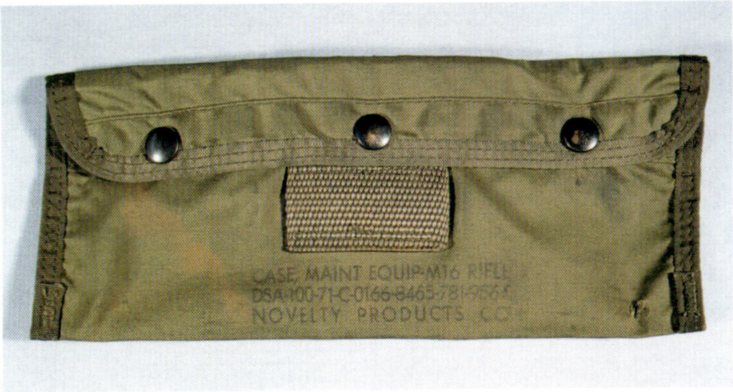

Close up of the Case Maintenance Equipment, M16, or "cleaning kit" for short. Inside would be a bore brush, cleaning rod, patches, and a tooth brush.

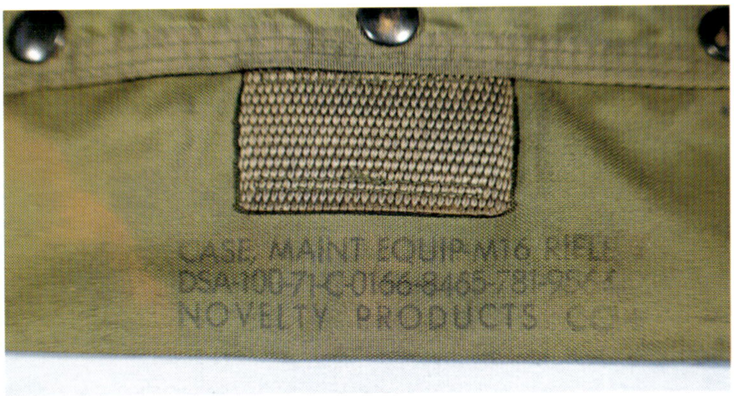

Close up of the date on the rifle cleaning kit labeled Case, Maint. Equip. M16 Rifle. DSA-100-71-C-0166.

round magazines with a single M26 grenade. Worn on his right side is an additional Small Arm pouch with another four 20 round magazines. The pouch holds one purple "Goofy Grape" M18 smoke and a single M26 grenade. Duct taped to the left side of his H harness is the SDU-5/E distress marker (Strobe Light) in its nylon case. On the right side is a single D-ring.

Rucksack is the nylon Tropical ruck nicknamed the jungle rucksack. Four prototypes arrived in Vietnam in 1965 for testing and evaluation. Soon another 500 Tropical rucksacks were ordered in 1966. In July 1967, the Tropical rucksack was adopted, but no procurement was made until the ACTIV evaluation report of 10 October 1967 was reviewed. By late 1968, the Tropical

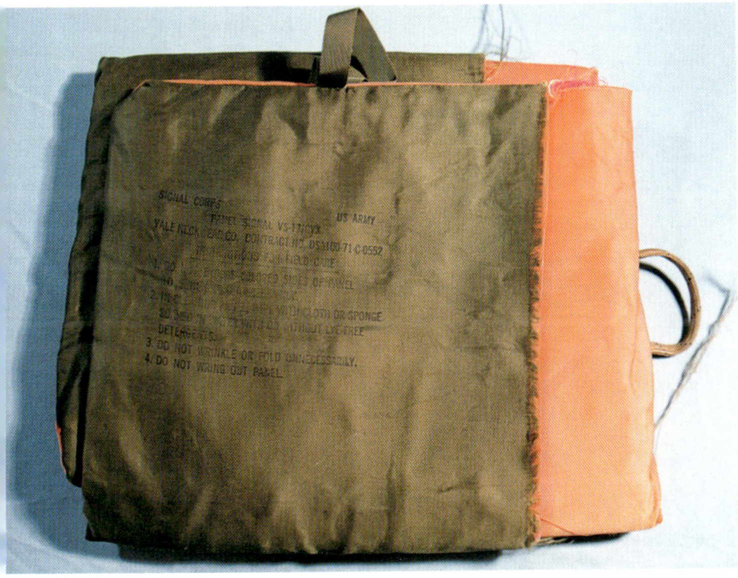

Close up of 1971 dated Panel, Signal, V-S-17/CVX. DSA 100-71-C-0552.

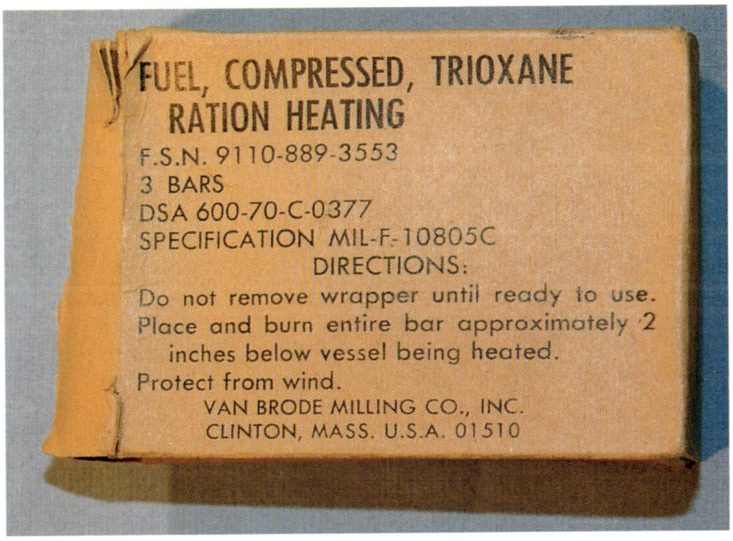

Close up showing a box of Heating fuel for cooking the C-Rats.

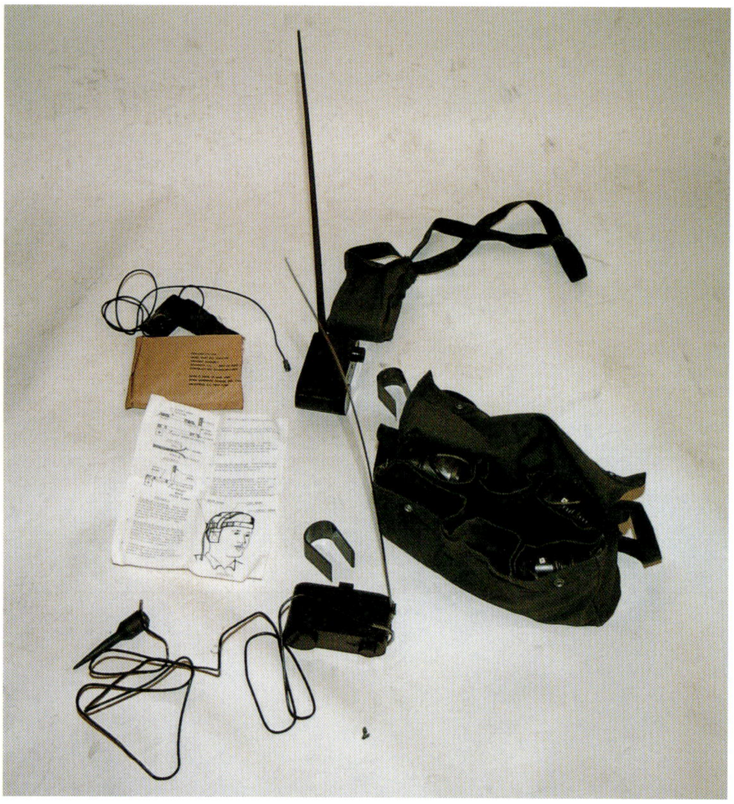

Layout of Trail monitoring device used by Rangers and Infantry alike.

Close up showing the Ranger removing a 20 round magazine from his M1956 canteen cover, which is used as an ammo pouch. Note the 2qt canteen turned around so the neck faces out and doesn't get in the way.

Close up of the final model 2qt canteen and cover. The canteen would remain the same from 1967 onward, and the cover was standardized by 1968.

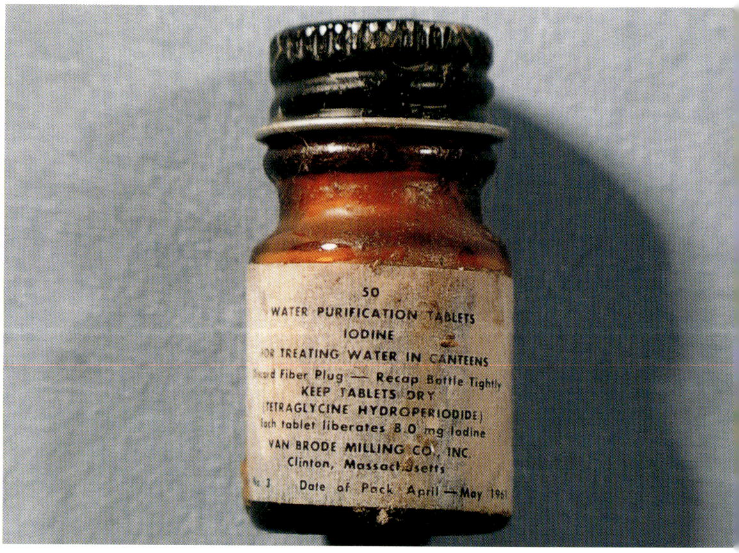

Close up showing the water purification bottle. Note the date, 1961.

Another close up showing the instruction label on the bottle of the water purification bottle.

Co L Ranger with black beret. Note the lack of any insignia or device on his black Ranger beret, which was not uncommon.

Co L Ranger enjoys himself during some much-deserved down time. Note the 4 year old "FM" Playboy magazine and the Montagyard bracelet.

rucksack became available to most combat troops. Attached to the right side of the ruck is a single 1qt canteen in the 1qt cover. Beneath that is a nylon 2qt carrier with the 2qt collapsible canteen. A single M18 smoke is fastened to the outside of the ruck. Connected to the left side is the 5qt collapsible flotation bladder, which was first produced in 1968 and "consisted of a 5-quart collapsible vinyl film bladder with nylon cover. The cover featured retainer loops and tie-down cords at each corner. A pocket was provided for holding water purification tablets, along with Instructional diagrams for filling the bladder that were printed directly on both sides of the cover."[78] "Connected to the center of the ruck is an M 18A1 Claymore anti-personnel mine with electric firing device M57, electrical test set M40 and wire."[79] Headgear is an OD green triangular bandage. In his hand he carries both an M16A1 with 30 round magazine and the M-79 grenade launcher.

Close up of final model Jungle boots with the "Panama" soles.

Ranger, Co. C Frank Benns sits on civilian table outside hooch at An Khe. Note the Co. C Ranger scroll on his left sleeve of his "Flower Powers" and the length of his mustache. July 1971. Courtesy (Frank Benns)

Jimi Hendrix of the Nam! All cammied up for a mission. Note the camera in his right hand. An Khe 1971. (Courtesy Frank Benns)

Two members of Franks Team, Co C before a mission. Note the M16 rifles and the 5qt-water bladder. An Khe 1971. (Courtesy Frank Benns)

Ranger of Co C all geared up prepares to move to the LZ before mission, An Khe 1971. Note the drive on rag used as a headband. (Courtesy Frank Benns)

Close up of Browning Hi-Power 9mm. Note there are two frames, this is because it was taken by a special EE pen camera, used by Rangers and Special Forces. (Frank Benns Collection)

"Ranger" Frank Benns all geared up. Note the fatigue shirt is tucked into trousers, and the headband made out of parachute material. Also, note the single "Recon" glove worn on his left hand. (Frank Benns Collection)

"Ranger" Frank Benns, in front of hooch. Note the ERDL shirt with Co C scroll wings and CIB, no name or Army strip present. 1970-71. (Frank Benns Collection)

Frank Benns in bunk, note socks pulled up over pant legs, full color scroll, and the addition of his name and a U.S. Army strip. He lays on a poncho liner. (Frank Benns Collection)

Co C Ranger returns fire from RON position. Note the tigerstripe uniform still in use in 1970-71. (Frank Benns collection)

Frank Benns with puppy outside of hooch. 1970-71. (Frank Benns collection)

Ranger E-5 outside Team area. Note the numerous grenade rings in his boonie, the white T-shirt, and the in-country made E-5 rank on his collar. 1971, An Khe C Co 1st Field Force. (Frank Benns collection)

Unidentified C Co. Ranger near Company area, evident by jeep and Connex boxes. This Ranger looks more like a Marine Recon member with his ERDL boonie hat and para nylon scarf. An Khe 1971. (Frank Benns Collection)

C Company ranger with black beret, note the subdued 1st Field Force patch and the subdued Ranger scroll, very unusual. (Frank Benns Collection)

C Company Ranger all cammied up and ready to go. Note the tigerstripe face paint to match his tigerstripe boonie hat. (Frank Benns Collection)

Ranger Sgt. stands next to Company jeep. Note the Ranger scrolls on both service side and combat side, along with metal E-5 rank pinned to his right shirt flap. On his black beret he wears a black and gold oval, a pair of pin back airborne wings, and a miniature Ranger scroll above the other two. Note the Ray Ban® sun glasses. An Khe, 1971. (Frank Benns Collection)

Good shot of C Co. Ranger and Ranger scroll on ERDL shirt. Note nothing is worn on his black Ranger beret. Quinhon Army Airfield, Vietnam, 1971.

Three rangers from Co C at the Quinhon Army Airfield. Two wear the black ranger beret with black and gold oval, while the ranger in the middle wears the black and gold oval on his baseball cap. 1971. (Frank Benns Collection)

Close up of Frank in an ERDL jacket showing airborne wings CIB and full color scroll. (Frank Benns Collection)

Company C Ranger sits on his bunk with guitar, An Khe 1971. (Frank Benns Collection)

C Co. Ranger enjoys his pipe on his bunk. Note the Ranger scroll is the "swallow tail" variation, and has turned pink. Underneath is a Vietnamese made 1st Field Force. 1971. (Frank Benns collection)

Co. C Ranger in ERDLs and ball cap. Note the ball cap is bare of wings or jump oval, and he also has a "swallow tail" Ranger scroll.1971. (Frank Benns Collection)

Four C Co. Rangers gather outside Ranger lounge. Note the two different ways the black beret is being worn here. One man (center) wears the oval and wings over his right ear, while the man behind him wears the black and gold ranger tab and wings over his left eye. 1971. (Frank Benns collection)

C Co. Ranger formation. Everyone seems to be on the same sheet of music with their berets being worn in the same manner. An Khe 1971. (Frank Benns collection)

Two heavily laden Rangers all geared up prepare to board choppers. Note the man on the left has a grenade vest, his M79 is cut down and stuffed inside his rucksack. Also note the word "LEG" painted in yellow on the brim of his hat. He holds three fingers that stood for WAR, while his buddy holds up the peace sign. (Frank Benns Collection)

Ranger sits and waits for mission. Unclear in photo, but his hat reads "F**k You I'm Dead!" (Frank Benns Collection)

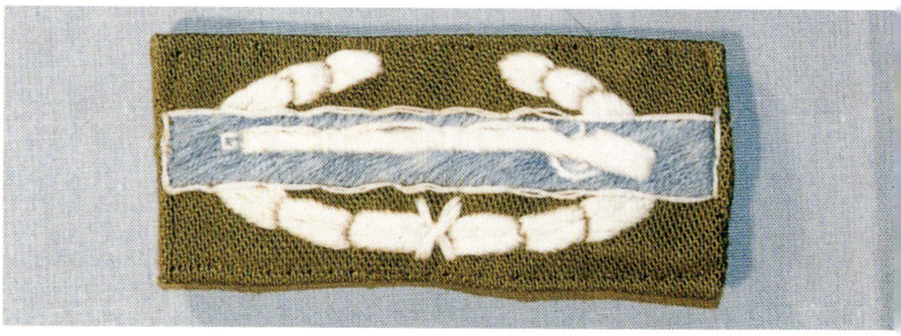

Close up of full color handsewn C.I.B. Vietnamese made.

Close up showing electric razor.

Great photo of 4 and a half Rangers from Co. C. Note only the one man has a CAR-15 "Shorty" with an M16 birdcage flash suppressor on it. Frank Benns said these were in great demand and hard to get one's hands on. Note the man on the left has a 30 round magazine in his M16A1 rifle—these were also hard to obtain. (Frank Benns Collection)

Full figure of 4th Bn, 21st Infantryman, 1971.

Full figure of "Gimlet." Note the minimal LBE worn at this time.

4th Battalion, 21st Infantry, 11th Brigade, "Gimlets," 23d Infantry Division
Duc Pho
Rifeman

"The 4th Battalion, 21st Infantry ('Gimlet') was activated 1 Nov. 1967 in Hawaii to serve as a fourth maneuver battalion of the 11th Infantry Brigade (Light). On 15 February 1969, the Battalion officially became part of the 23d Infantry Division (Americal)."[80]

This soldier typifies the ultra-lax attitude of the war in its final stages. His rip-stop fatigue shirt has been altered by the removal of the sleeves. In addition, he has also removed the U.S. Army strips from his left breast pocket. An M1956 pistol belt is worn, with a single M1967 Case small arms, nylon, with a single "baseball" grenade. On his left he carries a single canteen cover

Right: *Front View of Vietnamese made two pocket ERDL rip-stop shirt, intended for an ARVN Ranger or Airborne soldier. This one features a U.S. Army strip, along with 1st Field Force SSI and a Forward Observer "arc." Periodically, F.O.s were attached to Ranger units, this one was probably attached to Company C. (Courtesy Bob Chatt)*

Full figure rifleman from the 21st Infantry showing off with captured AK 47 rifle. Note the magazine is missing from his war trophy.

Full figure of Infantryman, holding up his new prize. Note the numerous grenade pins in his ERDL boonie hat.

FSB Buffalo, An Khe, RVN, April 1971. Sgt. Michael Belis in center. Co C 1stBn, 22nd Infantry, 1st Field Force Vietnam.

Close up of the Forward observer "arc," which is locally produced, along with the 1st FFV, which appears to be a U.S. made twill variation. Below it is a single U.S. produced E-5 chevron. (Courtesy Bob Chatt)

Close up showing additional material added to the shirt to make it a larger size for an American to wear. (Courtesy Bob Chatt)

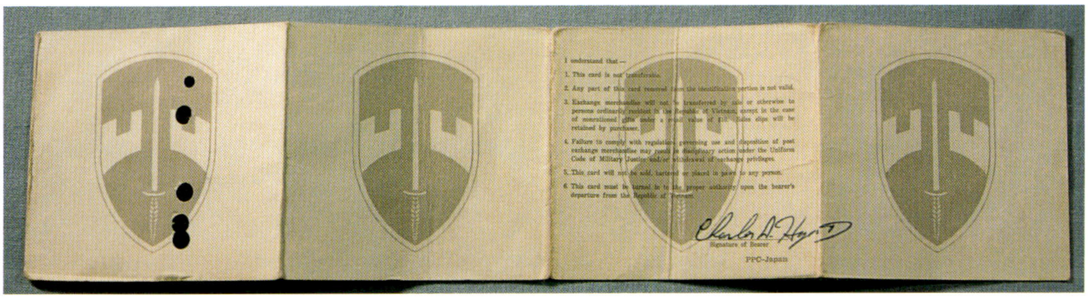

Close up showing MACV ration card, dated 1971.

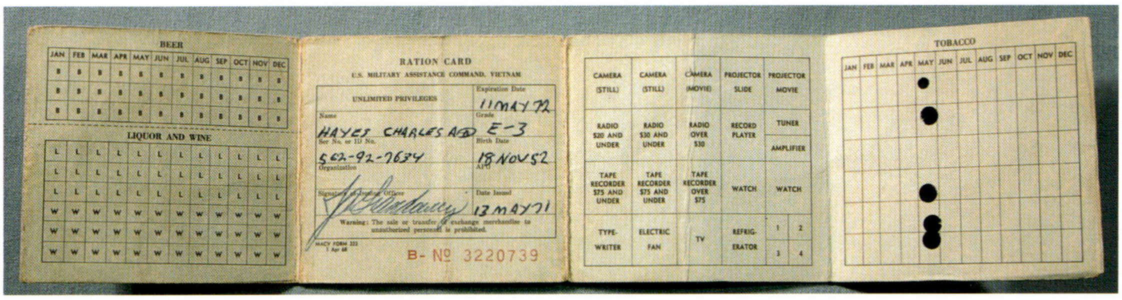

Close up of inside of Ration card.

8

At a Glance

Lightweight Rucksack w/aluminum frame. First issued 1963. (Arik Greenberg collection)

Backside of Lightweight Rucksack.

Backside of Tropical. Note the X frame.

Tropical Rucksack w/ steel X Frame. First issued 1968.

Close up of printed date on Tropical, DSA 100-68-C-2782.

Close up showing metal grommet. This was done away with by 1960. All early universal pouches have this grommet.

M1956 Universal pouch, sometimes called an M14 pouch by mistake. First issued 1956.

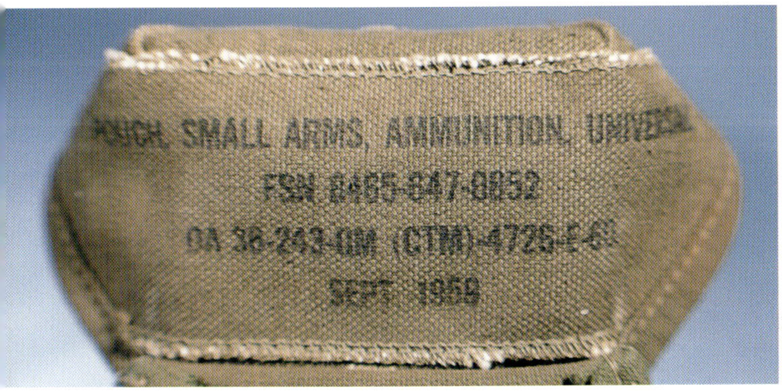

Close up of printed label inside. Sept 1959.

Post 1960 era M1956 Case Small Arms Ammunition, or Universal pouch. This model does not have the metal grommet.

Close up of printed label inside M1956 Case Small Arms Ammunition.

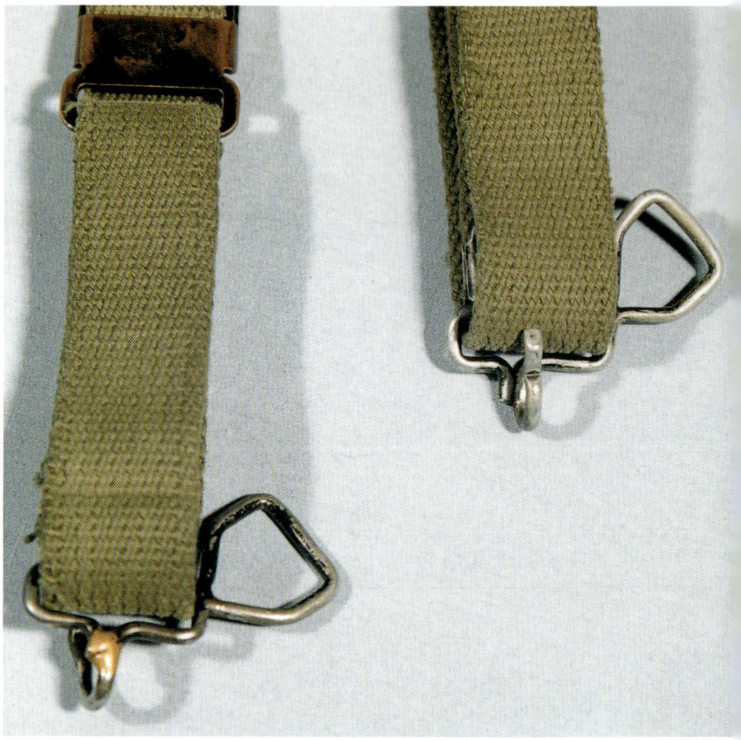

Close up showing the early model M1956 suspender clamps to secure H-harness to pistol belt. This would be replaced by the newer style by 1961.

M1956 Cotton H-Harness.

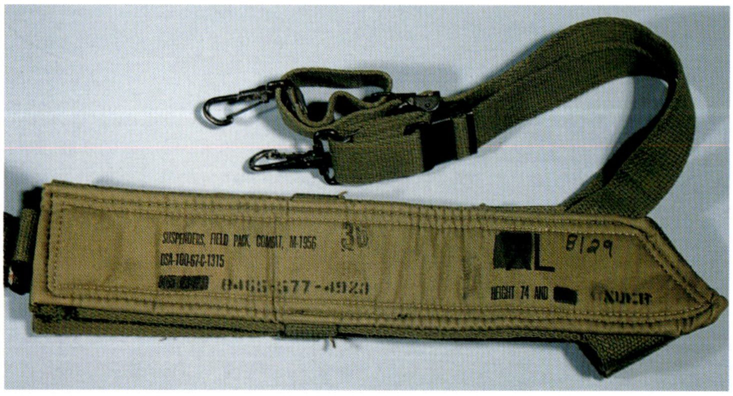

Close up of printed label on underside of H-harness. Size is XL, note the date DSA 100-67-C-1315.

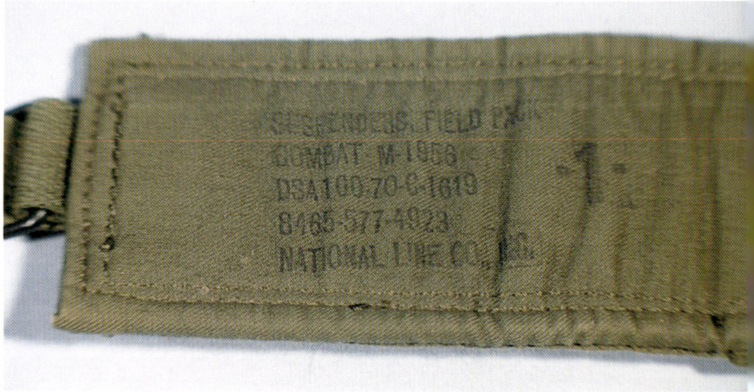

Close up showing the 1970 printed date of the underside of the cotton H-harness.

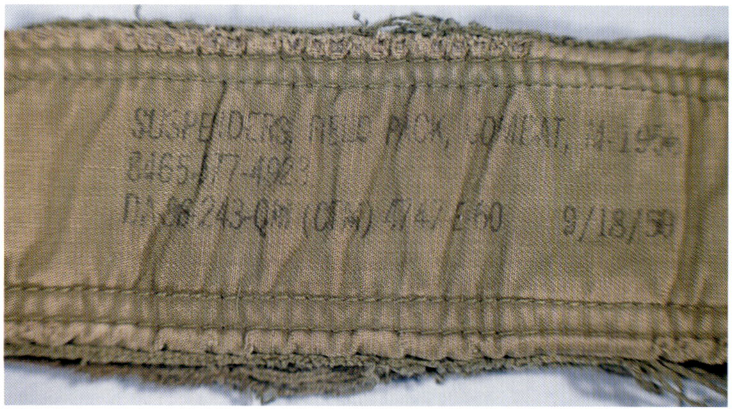

Close up of 1959 dated cotton Suspenders, Field Pack Combat, M1956; H-harness.

Close up of 1973 Suspenders, Field Pack Cotton, M1956. Note the underside is nylon coated. This began around 1972.

Pouch, Small Arms Ammunition Pouch M16A1. These began showing up late 1967, early 1968.

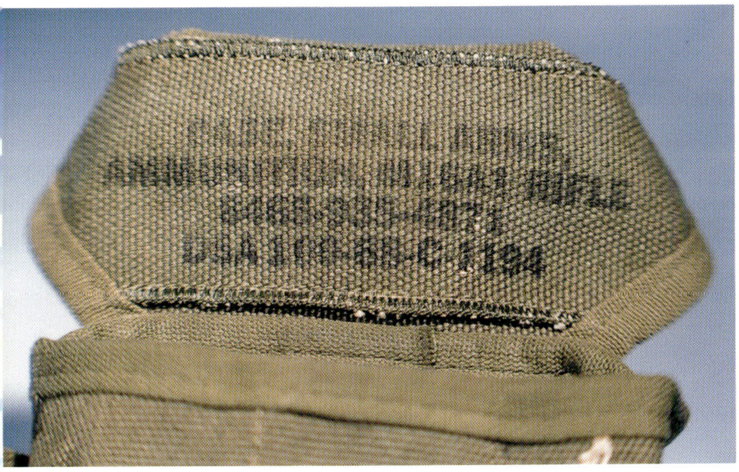

Close up of printed label, note the 1968 date.

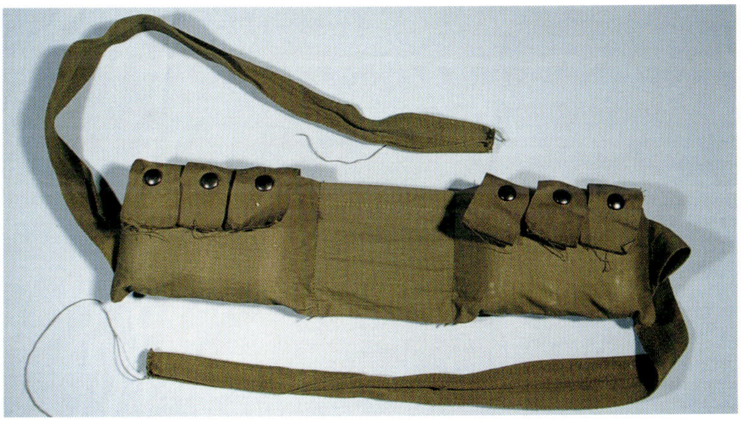

Early model M79 cotton bandoleer. Note the solid snap. This would be changed by 1969.

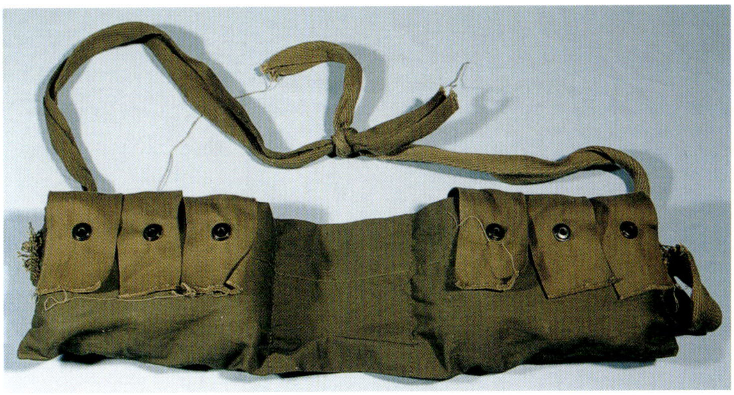

Post 69 M79 cotton bandoleer. Note the snaps have holes in them.

M18 Claymore bag. Note the solid snaps; these too would change in 1969-70 to the snap with the holes.

M1956 first aid/compass pouch with lensetic compass.

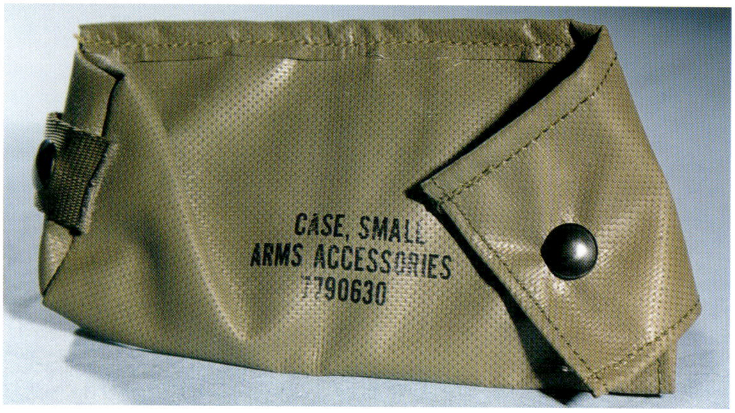

Case Small Arms Accessories, cleaning kit.

XM3Bi pod and Case, Carrying, Bipod 1970.

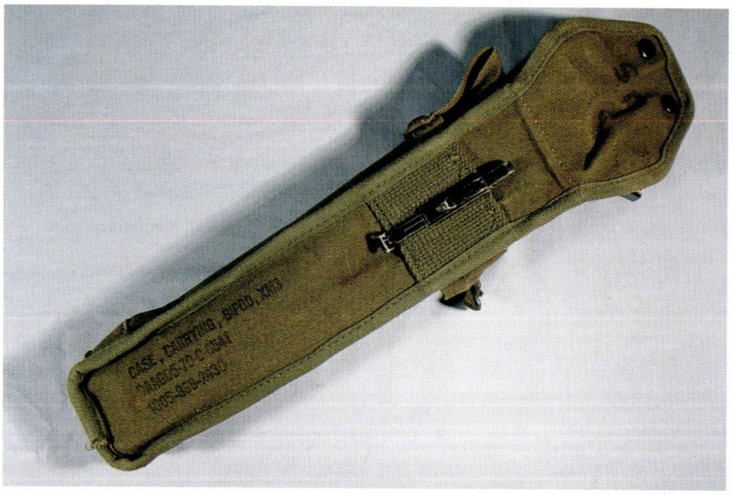

Back side of bipod case. Note the single "slide keeper."

Close up of printed label showing this one was produced in 1970.

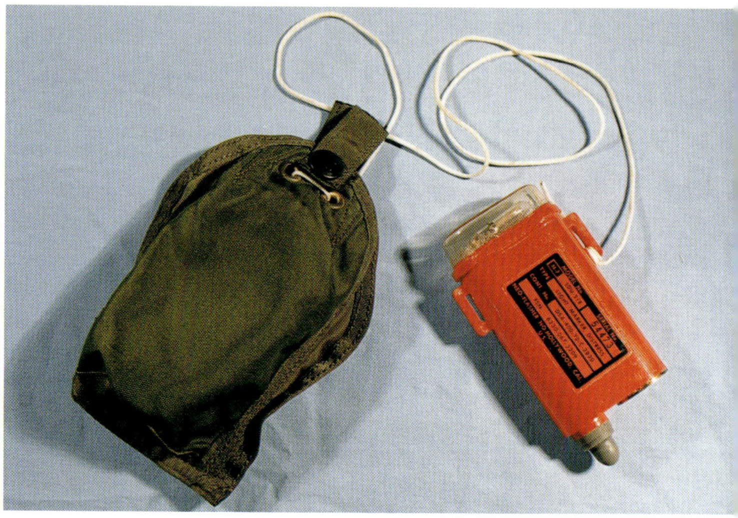

Light Marker Distress "strobe" SDU-5/E, and its nylon carrier. Note the entire strobe is orange. Later models have a black band along the top where the lens meets the body. The nylon cases are slightly different, also.

Nylon case for SDU-5/E

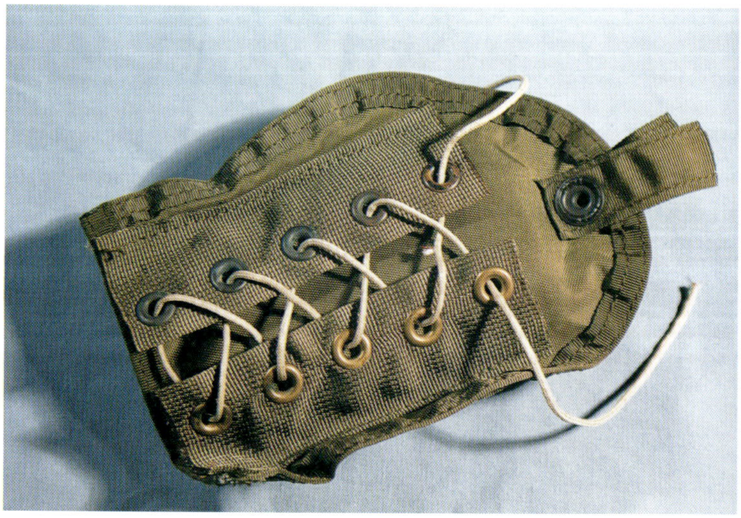

Backside of SDU-5/E Strobelight.

Close up of Panel Signal, VS-17/CYX, this one is dated 1971.

M1967 nylon Small Arms Ammunition Pouch M16, 20 Round. These began showing up in large numbers by 1968-69.

Close up of printed label of M1967 Small Arms Pouch. Note the date is 1968.

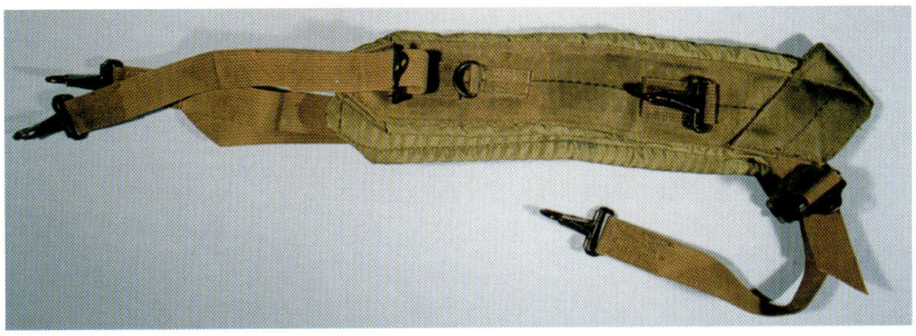

M1967 nylon Suspenders. Note the additional clips on it. The ALICE suspenders do not have this.

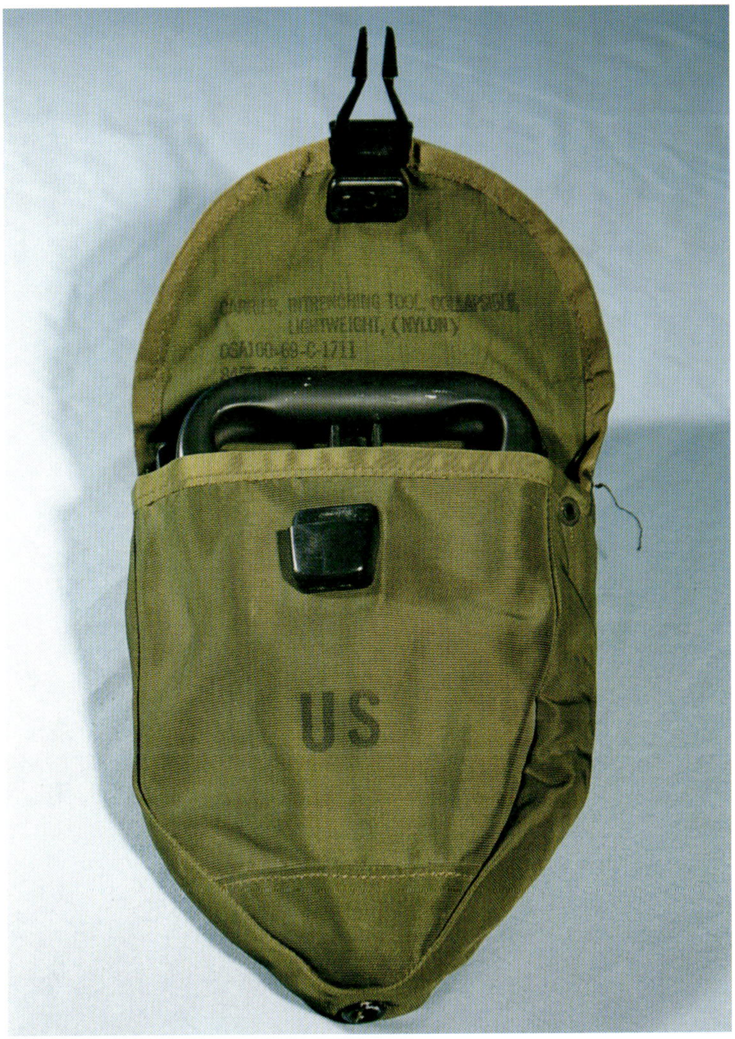

M1967 Lightweight Collapsible Entrenching tool and its nylon carrier. The carrier is dated 1969. These began arriving in Vietnam in large numbers by 1969-70.

M1967 nylon first aid/compass pouch.

M1967 nylon 1qt canteen cover.

Close up of printed label. Shows 1968 date.

1968 nylon 2qt canteen cover with 2qt canteen.

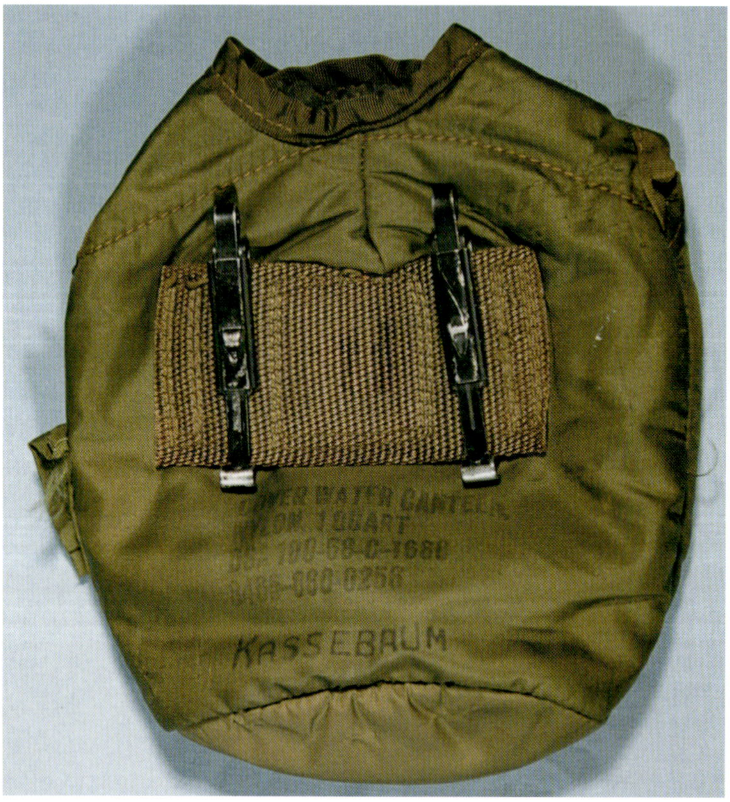

Back side of M1967 nylon 1qt canteen cover.

Back side of 1968 nylon 2qt-canteen cover.

Close up showing felt liner of 1968 era 2qt nylon canteen cover. Note the white cotton label inside the flap.

Example of two early 2qt canteens and covers. Right is the first model that was a WWII style that was upgraded for Special Forces in late 1961-62. The one on the left is the model that came out in early 1966.

1967 dated 2qt canteen. Note the "cobblestone" texture.

M1965 1qt canteen cover.

1968 dated 2qt canteen. Note the canteen is very smooth looking.

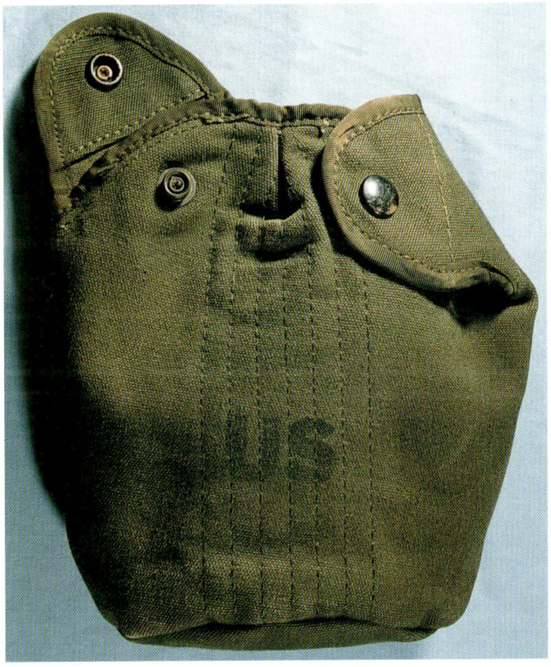

M1956 1qt canteen cover. By 1967 the M1956 cover was fitted with a nylon trim along the top.

Close up of printed label of 1967 era M1956 canteen cover.

30 Round Small Arms Ammunition case (M16 and M16E1 Rifle). Prototype cases were introduced in 1967, but due to problems with the 30 round magazines, cases like this were not standardized until 1969. Circa 1969.

Close up showing the '67 date.

Close up showing the cotton trim of the pre 1967 M1956 canteen cover, left, and the nylon trim that was introduced in 1967, on the right.

Close up showing plastic snap on the 30 round Small Arms Ammo Case (M16 and M16E1).

M1936 PISTOL BELT (KHAKI TAN)

M1944 PISTOL BELT (OG GREEN)

M1956 PISTOL BELT

M1965 PROTOTYPE W/ DAVIS FASTENER Horizontal Weave

M1966 PISTOL BELT COTTON Vertical Weave W/ Ball type fastener.

M1966 PISTOL BELT COTTON Vertical Weave W/ Prototype DAVIS FASTENER

M1967 NYLON PISTOL BELT W/ DAVIS FASTENER

(1968-69) M1967 NYLON PISTOL BELT W/Davis fastener (Note the difference in color)

Pistol Belt Development

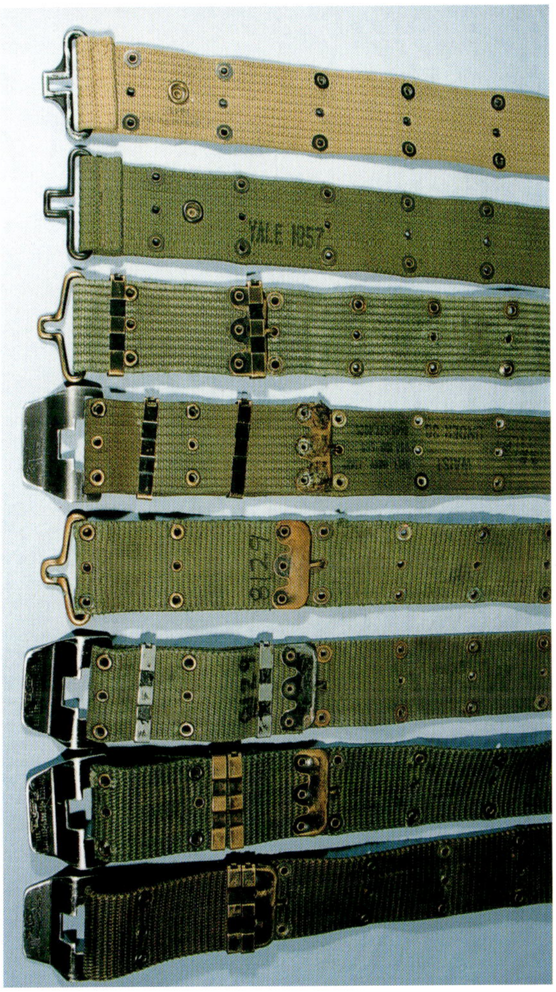

Backside (Left photo) *of pistol belts. Note the M1936 (Tan) and the M1944 (OD Green) can only be adjusted on the opposite end. Note also the metal snap.*

Opposite end backside (Right photo). *Note that some of the hardware is brass on some belts, while the M1966 vertical weave belt with the new Davis fastener features aluminum hardware.*

Close up showing the M1944 pistol belt with a 1957 date.

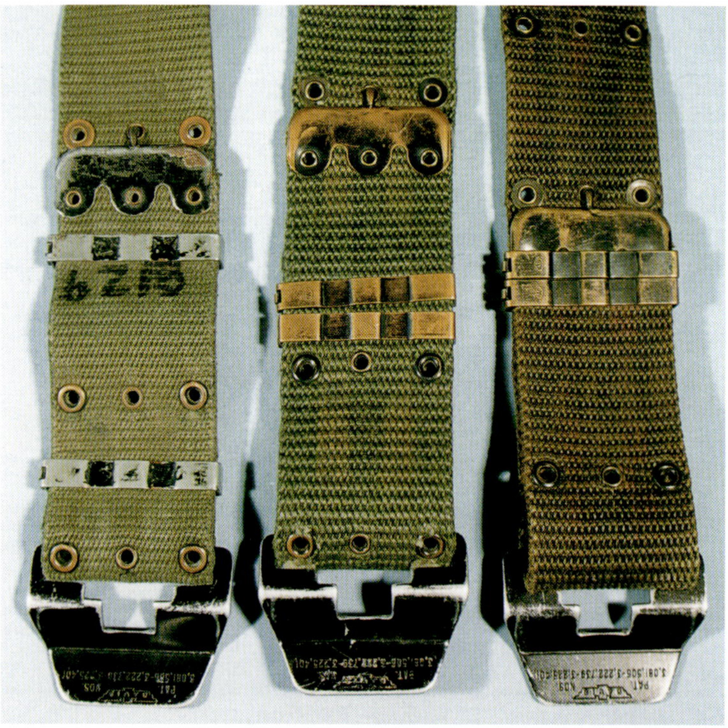

Close up showing from (left to right) the M1966 with Davis buckle, M1967 w/ Davis Buckle, and M1967 w/Davis buckle; note the difference in color between the two M1967 belts.

Close up showing the seam in the center of the 1967 ERDL Poncho liner. Post war production feature a similar pattern, but do not have this seam down the middle.

Close up showing tag on corner of Poncho liner. Note the '69 date.

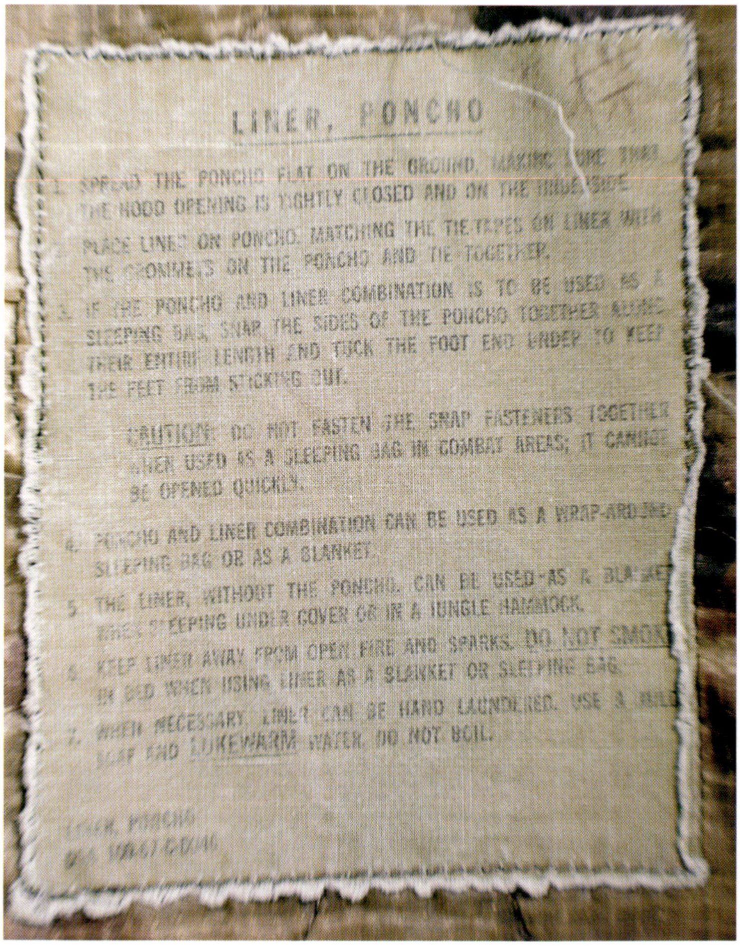

Close up of early 1967 dated Poncho liner tag. This is the first year of the ERDL Poncho liner. The years before were OD green, and before that they were "Duck Hunter" pattern.

TIME LINE OG 107 COTTON SATEENS: *1ST MODEL 1952* *2ND MODEL 12 APRIL 1963* *3RD MODEL 6 NOV. 1964*

Close up of pocket; First Model OG107.

Close up of Second Model Shirt pocket flap .

Close up of tag OG107 (CTM)-8863-C-61; shows this shirt was produced in 1961.

Close up of tag; Second Model; Shirt, Mans, Cotton, Sateen, Olive Green, Shade 107, 1-4848-65-C; '65 is the year produced.

Close up third model shirt pocket flap.

Close up of "Transitional Pattern," or "Delta pattern" ERDL trousers. These are neither the "Green" nor "Brown" Dominant pattern, but somewhere in between. One can begin to see these in 1969 and 1970.

Close up tag of third model shirt.

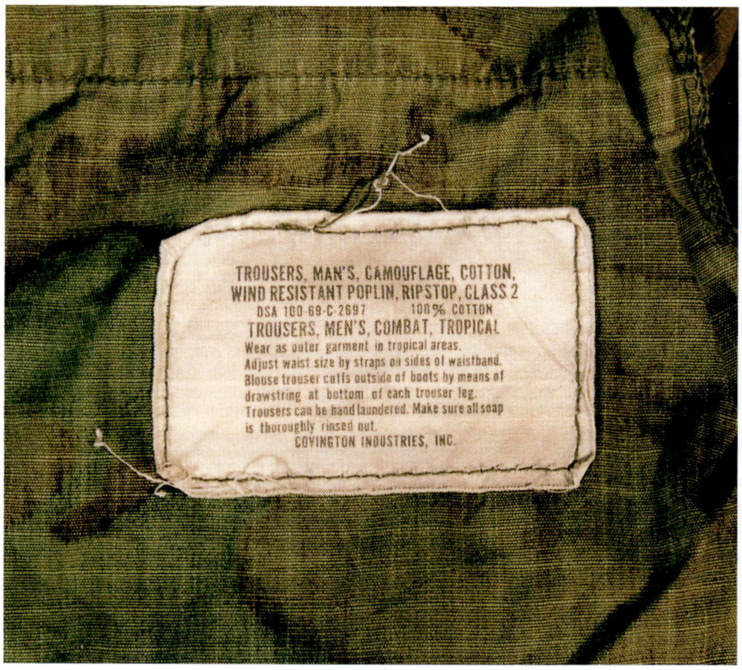

Tag of trousers proving they are truly ERDL and of wartime production.

Close up of tag and zipper fly of ERDL trousers.

Close up showing the zipper fly, another way of telling if they are wartime production. Note the white tag with the date is missing.

Close up of the small survival kit pocket that you will find in ALL Vietnam War time production ERDL trousers. This is in the left pocket only. Post war RDF trousers do not have this pocket.

Close up of cargo pocket of "Brown Dominant" trousers.

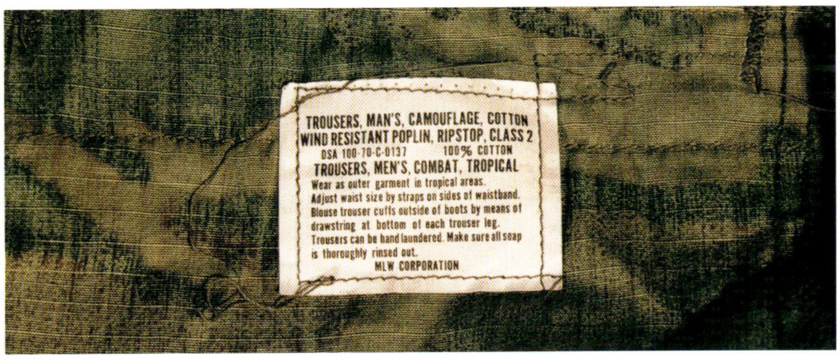

Close up of the tag that should be in the trousers. Note the date, 1970.

A.L.I.C.E.
(All-purpose Lightweight Individual Equipment)

The All-Purpose Lightweight Individual Carry Equipment is made up of components for the fighting load and additional components for the existence load. CONTRARY TO POPULAR BELIEF OR WHAT YOU HAVE HEARD, A.L.I.C.E. GEAR WAS NOT USED IN VIETNAM! Although certain pieces were tested in the late 1960s early 1970s, Alice gear never made it to Vietnam in any large amounts and was not issued out to troops, as was the M1956 and M1967 gear.

The following items and photos are used to help collectors, re-enactors, historians, and museum staff identify POST-War field gear, uniforms, and equipment, and not, in any way, to insult anyone's intelligence. This section is strictly for the novice and the beginner, and not intended for an ego trip on my end.

Up until now, artist renditions of uniforms in a popular English series showing Vietnam uniforms and equipment have been misleading, at no fault to the artist, who I deeply respect. So, many times paintings of the ERDL pattern uniform in both the Highland and Lowland pattern have been mistaken for the BDU uniform, the Lightweight uniform, and what I call the Rapid Deployment Force camouflage that came out in the late 70s and early 80s before the BDU uniform.

Also, the stitch pattern on nylon canteen covers and small minute details mean all the difference. I hope the following pages and photos will shed some light on what are Vietnam era gear and camouflage and what is NOT. And hopefully everyone will not make the same mistakes I made in the early years of collecting.

The ALICE PISTOL BELT is nylon, much like the M1967 pistol belt, but with one noticeable difference. The ALICE belt has only two rows of metal eyelets for the attachment of the old-style M1910 double-hooked items. Another noticeable feature of the Alice belt is the "Adjusting Clamp." Slide the adjusting clamp toward the belt buckle to loosen the belt and away from the belt to tighten it. Another giveaway is a new plastic buckle system. Just remember, three eyelets Vietnam era, 2 Post War.

THE MEDIUM FIELD PACK. ALICE has several characteristics that make it different from the Tropical Rucksack. First, it

ALICE Rucksack, without frame.

Backside of the ALICE rucksack. Note the lack of shoulder straps, the additional padding at the top, and the small window (Bottom) for the soldier to put his name and SSN in, the Tropical has neither of these.

Close up showing the ALICE metal snaps and the early metal fasteners.

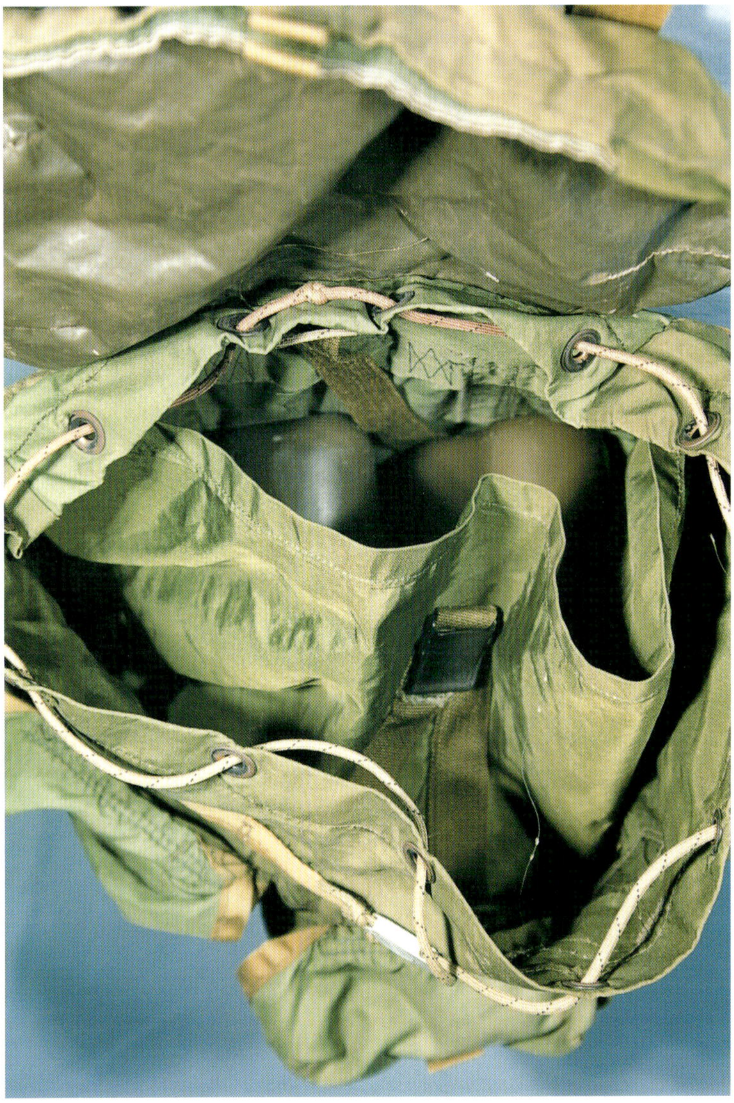

Close up showing the inside pocket of the ALICE intended for the PRC/77 radio. The Tropical is not compartmentalized, it has one large pocket.

has metal snaps, not plastic snaps, and secondly, the ALICE ruck has an inside pocket used to hold the PRC 77 radio (See Insert), while the Tropical does not. The shoulder straps can be removed from the ALICE, while on the Tropical Ruck, they're on there for life. Tropical has an integrated X-frame, made of steel. Alice's frame is aluminum and is tubular. The ALICE also comes in two sizes, Medium and Large. The large features three upper outside pockets and is considerably larger than the Med. The ALICE comes in six components, which are: Combat Field pack; pack frame; shoulder straps (2); lower back strap; waist strap (2); and kidney pad. There are additional items, such as a cargo support shelf, cargo tie-down straps, and a camouflage cover. The Tropical has none of these.

SMALL ARMS AMMUNITION CASES. Each of the small arms ammo cases (ALICE) hold three 30 round magazines (M-16), and the cases feature grenade pockets on each side and the plastic "squeeze catch" fastener. An early model of this was introduced in 1969, the only difference is the lack of grenade pockets; instead, there are the typical grenade "slots" similar to the universal pouch, secured with plastic snaps. Also, an early ALICE small arms case was introduced in 1973 much like the

Modern ALICE. Small Arms Pouch, M16.

Early model 1973 of the Small Arms Pouch, M16 with the 3 individual compartments.

current one, but each magazine was separated by its own compartment and covered.

2QT CANTEEN AND COVER. The newer 2qt collapsible canteens are easily distinguishable from the Vietnam era ones. The first difference is the date on the canteen itself, which appears on the center of the body of the canteen, along with the maker's name on the back with the slide keepers. The second is usually the cap, which is fitted with either a black or OD green apparatus for use with the M17A1 protective mask, so the user can drink water without removing his mask. On the cover, note there is a

Close up showing modern ALICE 2qt canteen and cover.

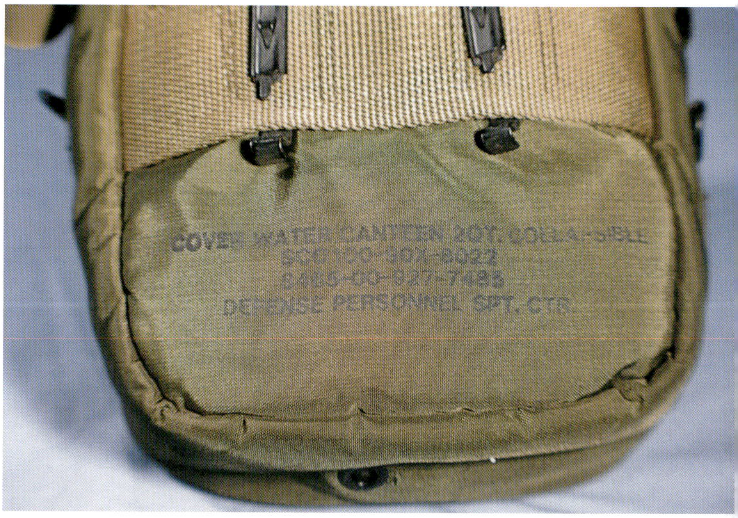

Backside of modern 2qt cover. The date appears in the number sequence SCC-100-90X-8022. This canteen cover can be identified as being produced in 1990.

A clear shot of the correct 2qt canteen and cover (Left) and the post war modern ALICE 2qt canteen and cover (Right). Note the small difference in the flap.

Close up showing the modern 2qt canteen. The maker's name and date are clearly on the canteen. U.S. SONETRONICS 1991.

Close up showing ALICE 2qt canteen with ALICE cover. Note the black M17 mask drinking apparatus on the 2qt canteen.

Comparison of ALICE canteen cover (left) and M1967 nylon canteen cover (Right).

minor difference on the shape of the flap (see insert). The cover is also heavier, due to the amount of fur lining, and the cover will be dated the same way as the Vietnam era covers, on the back below the retaining clips. On the new, the cover is a darker green.

Note the large green instruction label on the modern 2qt-canteen cover.

CANTEEN COVERS. The early ALICE covers look identical to the M1967 covers, except once again metal snaps have replaced the plastic snaps of the M1967 ones. They both feature four rows of vertical stitches. The second generation features only two rows, which are now horizontal. The cover on the left is a 1972 dated ALICE cover with a 1980s dated canteen. Note that the differences are very small.

FIRST AID DRESSING/COMPASS Pouch. The ALICE item has metal snaps, while the true M1967 has plastic snaps. The pouch on the (Right) is the M1967; note black plastic snap, the one on the (Left) ALICE Compass pouch.

ALICE SUSPENDERS. Alice are Y shaped, and there is only a single strap down the back. The true M1967 is identical to the H-harness, but in nylon with the addition of two fasteners for a light marching pack M1967 Nylon suspenders. The difference in the

BASEBALL CAPS; there are slight differences between the ball caps of post 1974 and the ball caps of pre-'74. The Wartime production cap features only TWO rows of stitching on its visor. It also features two ventilation-holes, near the top. The post war cap features FOUR rows of stitching and does not have the ventilation-holes on top in the front. Also note the slight difference in color. The one on the left is the post war, while the one on the right is a War-Time production. 1965.

Comparison of ALICE first aid/compass case (Left) and the nylon M1967 first aid/compass case w/ plastic snap (Right)

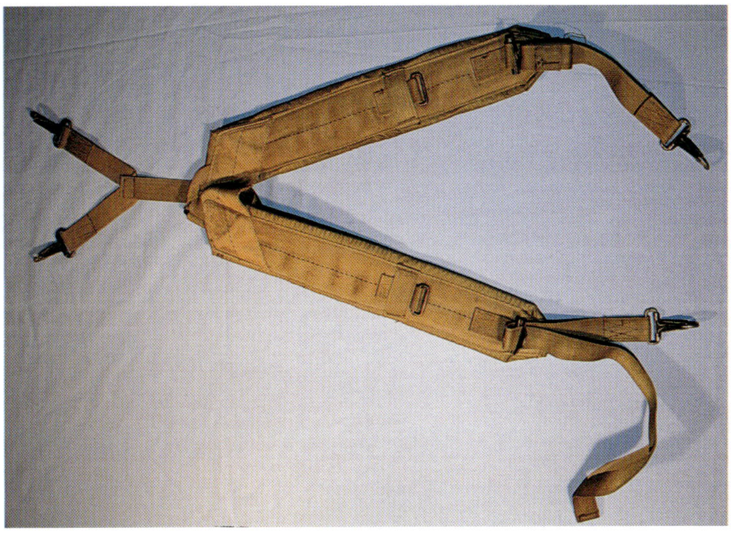

ALICE Suspenders. Note the Y shape. The M1967 nylon ones are H-shaped, like the H-harness.

Close up showing post war production Jungle boot. Note the Lack of the vertical stitch.

Close up showing the correct war time production Jungle boot, note the small vertical stitch. Other than a few minor differences, the modern jungle boots are almost identical to war time boots!

Close up of printed date on inside of nylon trim at the top of the boot. It reads, the boot size "10 R" then the date produced; Aug "8" of "65."

Close up showing tag from early Jungle boots, 1964. By the last month of 1965 this tag would disappear and be replaced with the printed tag.

M1967 nylon H-harness over ALICE Y-straps is an extra clip on the M1967 suspenders, and double straps running down the back.

INTRENCHING TOOL COVER: the Alice cover is either light green or dark forest green and made of plastic. The true nylon M1967 cover is green nylon.

M1967 Entrenching Tool Cover. Note that the wartime production is dated 1969, is all nylon, and features the "squeeze catch."

Jungle boots

Here is an easy way to distinguish War time production Jungle boots and Post War boots. First off, the early boots will have the "Vibram soles," that's the NON Panama Soles. There should be a date on the instep-side of the nylon strip at the upper most top, or, it will have a date on the "tongue" facing outward. In addition, you should look for a small vertical "stitch" up the heel. If you can identify these things, then you definitely have a set of the Wartime Production Jungle boots. You also want to look for the makers' names on the bottom next to the size, names like BATA, RO-SEARCH, GENESCO, and C.I.C. are just a few. If you do not find these distinguishing characteristics, then you may have some Korean or Chinese made copies. Jungle boots with the later "Panama soles" are identified the same way. Just look for the vertical stitch up the heel. The newer Post war Production jungle boot, issued after Wartime surplus ran out, are very hard to differentiate from the wartime Jungle boot. The easiest way to tell the difference is the one true "tell tale" difference, which is the lack of the vertical stitch up the heel of the boot. Another way to tell is of course the date on the nylon trim, or on the tongue. Sometimes on the early boots, along with the date will be printed "Spike Protective," but if the boots are too worn then this will be a problem and difficult to read. Another small detail worth mentioning is the stitch pattern that appears on the nylon reinforcement along the angle, known as the "ankle support strip." Post war boots will have a totally different stitch pattern than their wartime ancestors. Post war boots were only made with the Panama sole, so if you're not too sure, then I would suggest only buying Jungle boots with the

Joe Pizzini, Bravo Company, 4th Bn. 87th Infantry (Light) 25th Infantry Div. Note the ALICE first aid/compass pouch, along with the post war angle head flashlight with the guards on each side of the switch. Panama, 1987. (Author's Collection)

John Carpenter (right), B. Co. 4th Bn., 87th Inf. and Sgt. Harris (left) look over a map while lost in Japan, Nov. 1988. Note that J. Carpenter wears the Medium ALICE ruck with the ALICE E-tool cover, which is plastic. (Author's collection)

NON Panama soles, otherwise known as the "Vibram sole." If you have a pair of the post war boots, the differences are barley noticeable, and in my opinion can be worn if the collector cannot find war time boots in his size. Unless you happen to have a pair of the black nylon, "speed lace" jungle boots, which are not acceptable, and were first produced in 1993-1994.

B.D.U. Battle Dress Uniform and other POST-War Camouflage Patterns

"This is the Army's name for the current camouflage fatigue/duty uniform. The USMC calls it the Woodland pattern, or just 'Woodlands.' Both the Army and Marine Corps adopted this pattern in late 1981, and it was intended to replace all other field

Author on island of Lanai, Hawaii, wears BDU uniform and A.L.I.C.E. LBE. Note the two large pockets in front called S.A.W. pouches intended to hold the drums for the Squad Automatic Weapon. These are more often used to hold MREs and snacks than actual drums for the M249 SAW. (Author's collection)

The Author (Right) with his Platoon Sgt. and Mentor SFC. Glover. Note the ALICE suspenders and ALICE first aid/compass pouches.

Example of lightweight cotton rip stop BDU uniform shirt. Note the side take up tabs brought back in 1986. Circa 1990.

BDU Trousers, note the makers have gone back to the 3 pleat system. These are very heavy and feel very much the same as the M1951 Field Trousers.

clothing. The uniform is made out of 50/50 nylon cotton fabric for greater burn protection. The uniform was the subject of criticism even before its first real 'combat test' on the island of Grenada. Some odd features of its styling, as well as the fabric itself, made it hot and uncomfortable in warm climates."[81] A lightweight Tropical BDU uniform was developed, but would not be issued to Army troops until 1987-88, when all Army Troops were required to buy two sets, if they had not already been issued them as part of their "Initial Issue" during Basic Training. The new lightweight BDU uniform was known in the Army as the "Lightweights." The first model BDU uniform had an outrageous "butterfly" collar, sometimes referred to as the "Elvis" collar. The second generation, which came into existence in early 1986, had done away with the ridiculously large collar, and now featured take up tabs on the side to give it a more slim appearance. The Author only wore the Lightweight uniform during his unit's deployment to Panama for JOTC, when the entire Battalion was issued three sets of the new Lightweight uniform, which was produced in cotton rip-stop.

Comparison of the Green Dominant ERDL trousers (Left) to the modern day BDU trousers in heavy weight material (Right). Note the size differences in the cargo pockets and the shape of the pocket flap. Also note that the ERDL is "rip-stop."

Comparison of the Green Dominant ERDL shirt (Left) to the Lightweight BDU uniform shirt in "rip-stop" (Right). Once again, note the differences in pocket size and number of pleats.

Author with machete in Panama wearing the lightweight woodland pattern BDU, along with a 1944-dated machete in a 1967-dated sheath. 1987.

He found the new uniform when brand new was so dark that it was like wearing black on a hot day—the sun seemed to bake you in them. When wet, they were more prone to tear, and after a 5-7 day field problem, you usually had duct tape holding them together. The heavier BDU uniform was much more comfortable after about 6 months of continuous washing and wearing, and once the item was broken in, they were like your favorite pair of old jeans, and would hold up through the entire field problem. The author still has BDU uniforms issued to him in 1986 that still fit and are still considered "serviceable," meaning no large holes after 13 years of "Wear & Tear." One good thing about the

Author (Right) with buddy Collin "Alf" Calsyn (Left) in 1988, East Range, Hawaii. Some units were still wearing the OG 107 uniforms at this time. Note the M16A1 rifles are also still in use. (Authors Collection)

Author in Panama wearing a 1973 dated M79/203 vest, and the lightweight woodland pattern BDUs.

Author (Right) with Large ALICE and S.A.W. stands next to SFC. Glover and a Cobra Helicopter. Both wear the BDU uniform. Japan, 1988.

Sgt. Jeffery Lassiter (center) wearing the brown post war T-shirt, BDU trousers, and fingerless black gloves during training at "Hungry Lizard" California, 1987. Note the man in the back with the scarf on his head and the grenade vest. (Authors collection)

Lightweight uniforms was they really looked sharp after a ton of starch and a good ironing!

Rapid Deployment Force Camouflage (HOT WEATHER, MEN'S CAMOUFLAGE PATTERN)

This pattern of camouflage is called the RDF pattern, named for the organizations that were issued it, such as the Marine Corps, and 101st and 82nd Airborne. The Rapid Deployment Force camouflage was introduced some time in the late 1970s-early 1980s and is very similar to the ERDL patterns. The RDF has a more NATO tone to it; the colors reflect the uniforms camo schemes of Europe. The RDF camo has a four pocket shirt that features a single pleat and no longer features the two upper breast pockets at a slant; they now match the two lower pockets, and are square

The Author (Right) shaking hands with the Secretary of the Army, the Honorable John. O. Marsh. Note the Author wears the BDU uniform and the Secretary wears the RDF camouflage. Big Island, Hawaii, 1986.

Close up showing post war RDF shirt pockets.

Close up showing right side of post war RDF camouflage shirt, note square pockets and their placement. Note material is the "Transitional," or "Delta" pattern ERDL, which has a kind of washed out look. Another example of correct material, incorrect cut.

and not rounded off. EVEN IF THE TAG IN THE COLLAR HAS BEEN REMOVED, YOU WILL PROBABLY STILL BE ABLE TO SEE THE STITCHING. The matching trouser feature a button fly, replacing the zipper fly of war time camouflage garments, and feature a new style of cargo pockets with a single pleat in the middle, unlike the 3 pleats of the garments before. Another way to tell the difference is the large tag on the inside that gives the sizes and date. If this is removed, then you should check for: first, Color; second, Button fly; third, Single Pleat cargo pocket; and fourth, IF THE TROUSERS ARE MISSING THE LITTLE POCKET WITH A SINGLE BUTTON INSIDE THE LEFT CARGO POCKET, the trousers you have are DEFINITELY POST WAR production. None of the newer trouser have this pocket, ONLY the WAR TIME Trouser have this pocket. Therefore, if you are unsure or uncertain about the pants for any reason, this is the decisive factor!

A SPECIAL NOTE: Companies like MLW Corporation, Covington Industries, did not make uniforms after the war. Beware, some companies used existing material such as the green dominant ERDL to make uniforms for the Government. Therefore, you might find a shirt or trouser with the correct material, but wrong cut. Also, Vietnam Uniforms DO NOT, I repeat, DO NOT have NATO SIZES. Here is a small list of Companies who got Government contracts for uniforms after the war:

Winfield MCG Co. INC.
Caribbean Needle Point, INC.
Guls Apparel Corporation, Dallas Uniform Division.
Proper International, INC. Carbon Hill Manufacturing CO. INC.

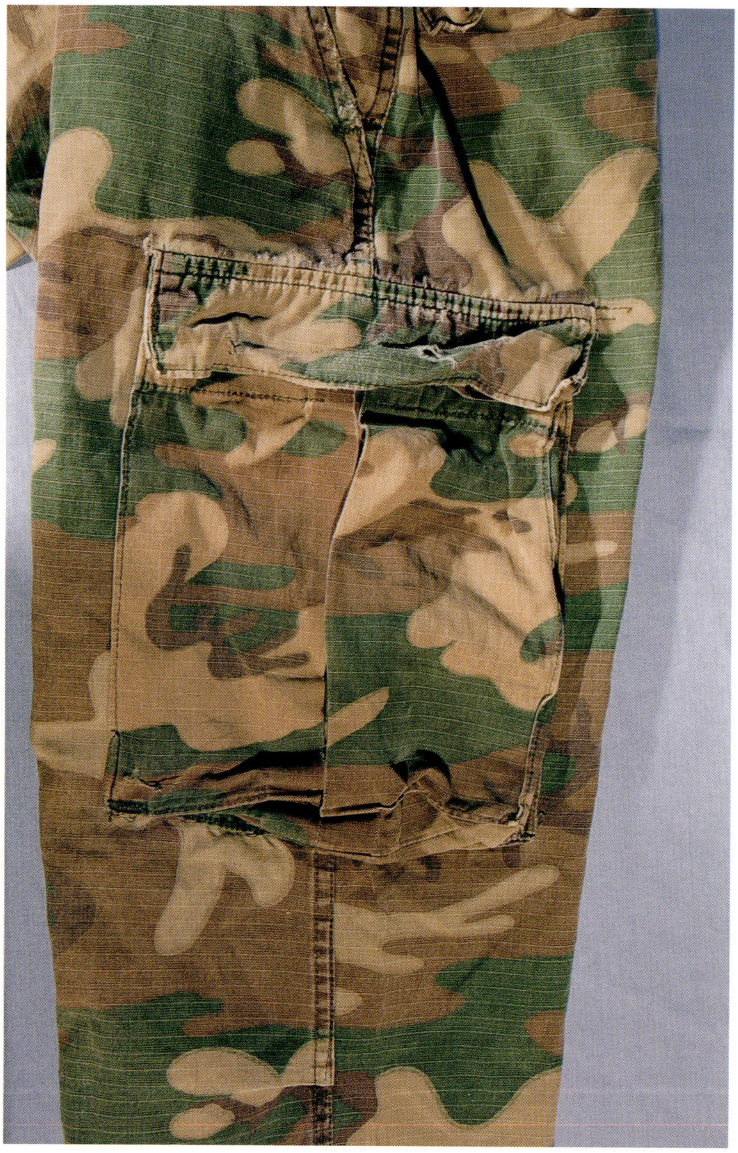

Example of RDF trousers in the Transitional/Delta Pattern. Note the single pleat in the center of the cargo pocket.

Close up of another example of RDF pocket. Note that this uniform's material is the "Highland."

Tailor tag from Trousers, Hot Weather Mens, Camouflage Pattern. This date shows they were produced in 1977.

Brown Dominant ERDL pattern. Another example of correct material, incorrect cut and dates.

Example of RDF trousers in the "Brown Dominant" pattern material, but seen here with the wrong pocket.

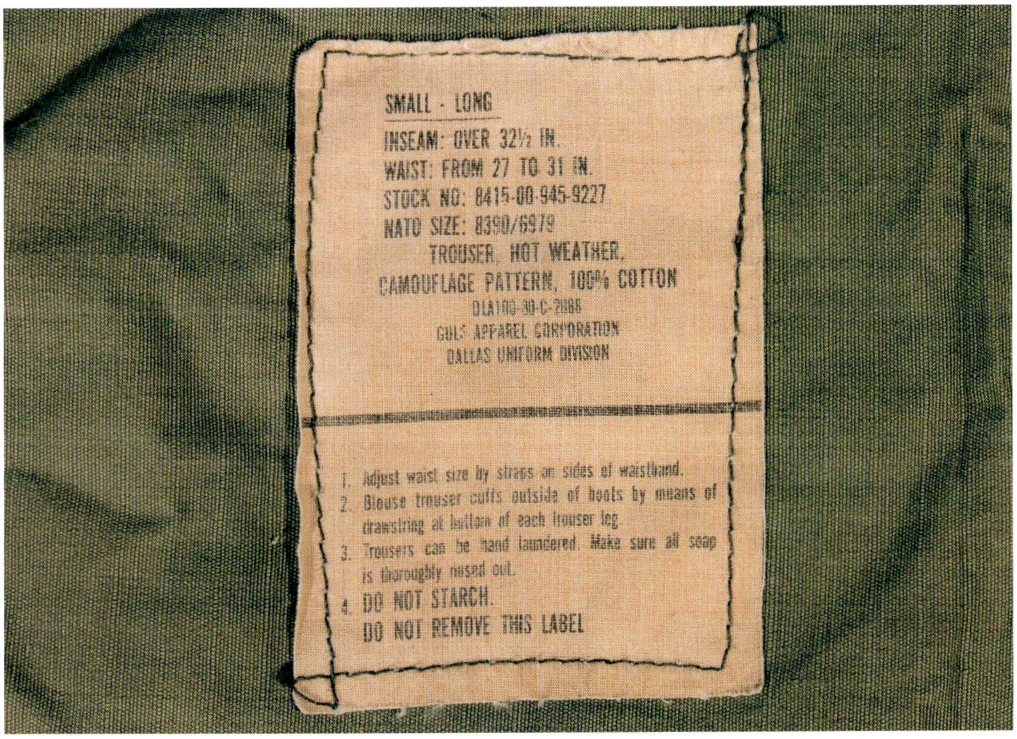

Tailor tag from the RDF showing NATO size: 8390/6979. Below is a description of the garment, Trouser, Hot Weather, Camouflage Pattern, 100% Cotton. And below the date, DLA100-80-C-2866, showing these were produced in 1980.

A good example of the correct pattern being used but incorrect date and cut. Note the cargo pocket, button fly, and camo "gas flap" in the opening. Special NOTE: the very first ERDL camouflage Trousers, produced in POPLIN, not rip stop, had a button fly, but only in cotton poplin.

Another example of the RDF camouflage trousers with incorrect pocket.

Close up of button fly and small gas flap on RDF trousers. Wartime production ERDL in "rip-stop" has a zipper fly and no "gas flap."

Comparision of "Green Dominant" ERDL (Left) and the Postwar RDF (Right). Note the difference in the pocket and pocket flap. Another method of identifying is to look for the small "survival kit" pocket in the left leg of the war time production of the uniform. If you don't find it you probably have a Post war piece.

Another comparison of the war time production (Left) and post war RDF camouflage trousers (Right).

Two correct ERDL trousers both produced during the war. The set on the (Right) is the "Transitional Pattern" ERDL, or "Delta" pattern. The other one (Left) is the "Green Dominant" ERDL. This is the most common pattern.

Notes

Chapter 1

[1] Stanton, Shelby, Rise And Fall of an American Army; (Navto, CA, Presidio Press, 1985), pp 49

[2] Stanton, Shelby, US Army Uniforms of the Vietnam War, (Harrisburg, PA, Stackpole Books,1988), pp 76

[3] Stanton, Shelby, US Army Uniforms of the Cold War 1948-1973, (Mechanicsburg, PA, Stackpole Books, 1994), pp 130

[4] Stanton, Shelby; US Army Uniforms of the Vietnam War; (Harrisburg, PA, Stackpole Books, 1988), pp 225

[5] Stanton Shelby; US Army Uniforms of the Vietnam War; (Harrisburg, PA, Stackpole Books, 1988), pp 151

[6] Stanton, Shelby; Rise and Fall of an American Army, (Navato, CA, Presidio Press, 1985), pp 56

[7] Lyles, Kevin; Vietnam: US Uniforms in Colour Photographs, (London W1, Windrow & Greene Ltd. 1992), pp17

[8] Stanton, Shelby; Rise and Fall of an American Army, (Navato, CA, Presidio Press, 1985), pp45

[9] Stanton, Shelby, US Army Uniforms of the Vietnam War, (Harrisburg, PA, Stackpole Books, 1988), pp 62, 65

[10] Stanton, Shelby U.S. Army Uniforms of the Vietnam War, (Harrisburg, PA, Stackpole Books, 1988), pp 65

Chapter 2

[11] Stanton, Shelby; Vietnam Order of Battle, (New York, Galahad Books, 1986) pp74

[12] Stanton, Shelby, The Rise and Fall of an American Army, (Navato, CA, Presidio Press, 1985)pp69

[13] Stanton, Shelby; Vietnam Order of Battle, (New York, Galahad Books, 1886)pp10

[14] Stanton, Shelby; U.S. Army Uniforms of the Vietnam War, (Harrisburg, PA, Stackpole Books, 1988), pp 167-168

[15] Lyles, Kevin, Vietnam: US Uniforms in Colour Photographs, (London W1, Windrow & Greene, 1992), pp33

[16] Stanton, Shelby, US Army Uniforms of the Vietnam War, (Harrisburg, PA, Stackpole Books, 1988), pp172

[17] Stanton, Shelby, Rise and Fall of an American Army, (Navato, CA, Presidio Press, 1985), pp 109-110

[18] Stanton, Shelby; US Army Uniforms of the Cold War; 1948-1973, (Mechanicsburg, PA, Stackpole Books, 1994), pp 166

Chapter 3

[19] Stanton, Shelby; Rise and Fall of an American Army, (Navato, CA, Presidio Press, 1985), pp97

[20] Stanton, Shelby, US Army Uniforms of the Vietnam War, (Harrisburg, PA, Stackpole Books, 1988), pp 65

[21] Cutler, Thomas J.; Brown Water, Black Beret, (Annapolis, Maryland, Naval Institute Press,1988)pp236-7

[22] Smyth, Cecil, U.S. Coastal Forces, Vietnam, 1984 pp17

[23] Cutler, Thomas J. Brown Water, Black Beret, (Annapolis, Maryland, Naval Institute Press, 1988)pp237

[24] Lyles, Kevin, Vietnam: US Uniforms in Full Color Photographs, (London W1, Windrow & Greene, 1992) pp 37

[25] Lyels, Kevin, Vietnam: US Uniforms in Colour Photographs, (London W1, Windrow & Greene, 1992), pp 37

[26] Lyles, Kevin, Vietnam: US Uniforms in Colour Photographs(London W1, Windrow & Greene, 1992), pp 24

[27] Stanton, Shelby, Rise and Fall of an American Army, (Navato, CA, Presidio Press, 1985), pp168-171.

[28] Stanton, Shelby U.S. Army Uniforms of the Vietnam War, (Harrisburg, PA, Stackpole Books, 1988), pp153-154.

[29] Stanton, Shelby; US Army Uniforms of the Vietnam War, (Harrisburg, PA, Stackpole Books, 1988), pp 156

[30] TM3-4240258-14

Chapter 4

[31] Stanton, Shelby; Rangers at War, (New York, Ivy Books, 1992), pp218-219

[32] Stanton, Shelby U.S. Army Uniforms of the Vietnam War, (Harrisburg, PA, Stackpole Books, 1988), pp8

[33] Stanton, Shelby U.S. Army Uniforms of the Vietnam War, (Harrisburg, PA, Stackpole Books, 1988), pp9-10

[34] Stanton, Shelby; Vietnam Order of Battle, (New York, Galahad Books, 1886)pp88

[35] Stanton, Shelby; Vietnam Order of Battle, (New York, Galahad Books, 1886)pp136

[36] Stanton, Shelby; Vietnam Order of Battle, (New York, Galahad Books, 1886)pp89

[37] Stanton, Shelby; Vietnam Order of Battle, (New York, Galahad Books, 1886)pp89

[38] Stanton, Shelby U.S. Army Uniforms of the Vietnam War, (Harrisburg, PA, Stackpole Books, 1988), pp5-6

[39] Lyels, Kevin, Vietnam: US Uniforms in Colour Photographs, (London W1, Windrow & Greene, 1992), pp 37

[40] Stanton, Shelby, Rangers at War, (New York, Ivy Books, 1992), pp154

Chapter 5

[41] Renosa, Mark, U.S. Combat Helmets of the 20th Century, (Atglen, Pa, Schiffer, 1997)

[42] Stanton, Shelby U.S. Army Uniforms of the Vietnam War, (Harrisburg, PA, Stackpole Books, 1988), pp183

[43] Stanton, Shelby U.S. Army Uniforms of the Vietnam War, (Harrisburg, PA, Stackpole Books, 1988), pp183

[44] Stanton, Shelby U.S. Army Uniforms of the Vietnam War, (Harrisburg, PA, Stackpole Books, 1988), pp26

[45] Stanton, Shelby U.S. Army Uniforms of the Vietnam War, (Harrisburg, PA, Stackpole Books, 1988), pp56

[46] Rottman, Gordon, Vietnam Airborne, (London, England, Osprey Publishing, 1990) pp18-20.

[47] Lyels, Kevin, Vietnam: US Uniforms in Colour Photographs, (London W1, Windrow & Greene, 1992), pp75

[48] Lyels, Kevin, Vietnam: US Uniforms in Colour Photographs, (London W1, Windrow & Greene, 1992), pp 75

[49] Stanton, Shelby U.S. Army Uniforms of the Vietnam War, (Harrisburg, PA, Stackpole Books, 1988), pp 227

[50] Stanton, Shelby U.S. Army Uniforms of the Vietnam War, (Harrisburg, PA, Stackpole Books, 1988), pp 227

[51] Lyels, Kevin, Vietnam: US Uniforms in Colour Photographs, (London W1, Windrow & Greene, 1992), pp 53

[52] Lyels, Kevin, Vietnam: US Uniforms in Colour Photographs, (London W1, Windrow & Greene, 1992), pp 46

[53] Stanton, Shelby U.S. Army Uniforms of the Vietnam War, (Harrisburg, PA, Stackpole Books, 1988), pp 214

[54] Stanton, Shelby, Rangers at War, (New York, Ivy Books, 1992), pp224-226

[55] Lyels, Kevin, Vietnam: US Uniforms in Colour Photographs, (London W1, Windrow & Greene, 1992), pp 59

[56] Stanton, Shelby, Rangers at War, (New York, Ivy Books, 1992), pp38

[57] Stanton, Shelby, Rangers at War, (New York, Ivy Books, 1992), pp38

[58] Stanton, Shelby, Rangers at War, (New York, Ivy Books, 1992), pp39

[59] Stanton, Shelby, Rangers at War, (New York, Ivy Books, 1992), pp123-127

Chapter 6

[60] AUTHOR - You asked for a footnote insert, no footnote listed at "58A" in edited manuscript - please provide

[61] Lyels, Kevin, Vietnam: US Uniforms in Colour Photographs, (London W1, Windrow & Greene, 1992), pp78

[62] Stanton, Shelby, Rise and Fall of an American Army, (Navato, CA, Presidio Press, 1985), pp 344-345

[63] Stanton, Shelby, Rangers at War, (New York, Ivy Books, 1992), pp186-187

[64] Stanton, Shelby, Rangers at War, (New York, Ivy Books, 1992), pp188-189

[65] Stanton, Shelby; Vietnam Order of Battle, (New York, Galahad Books, 1886)pp148

[66] Rottman, Gordon, Vietnam Airborne, (London, England, Osprey Publishing, 1990) pp6-8.

[67] Stanton, Shelby; Vietnam Order of Battle, (New York, Galahad Books, 1886)pp148

[68] Stanton, Shelby U.S. Army Uniforms of the Vietnam War, (Harrisburg, PA, Stackpole Books, 1988), pp 157-158.

[69] Stanton, Shelby, Rangers at War, (New York, Ivy Books, 1992), pp146-147.

[70] Stanton, Shelby, Rangers at War, (New York, Ivy Books, 1992), pp149-150.

[71] Stanton, Shelby, Rise and Fall of an American Army, (Navato, CA, Presidio Press, 1985), pp 349-341

[72] Stanton, Shelby, Rise and Fall of an American Army, (Navato, CA, Presidio Press, 1985), pp 341

[73] Stanton, Shelby, Rangers at War, (New York, Ivy Books, 1992), pp127-128.

Chapter 7

[74] Stanton, Shelby U.S. Army Uniforms of the Vietnam War, (Harrisburg, PA, Stackpole Books, 1988), pp 113.

[75] Stanton, Shelby, Rangers at War, (New York, Ivy Books, 1992), pp145.

[76] Stanton, Shelby, Rise and Fall of an American Army, (Navato, CA, Presidio Press, 1985), pp356

[77] Stanton, Shelby, Rangers at War, (New York, Ivy Books, 1992), pp173-174.

[78] Stanton, Shelby U.S. Army Uniforms of the Vietnam War, (Harrisburg, PA, Stackpole Books, 1988), pp173-174.

[79] Lyels, Kevin, Vietnam: US Uniforms in Colour Photographs, (London W1, Windrow & Greene, 1992), pp95

[80] Stanton, Shelby; Vietnam Order of Battle, (New York, Galahad Books, 1886)pp144
Stanton, Shelby; Vietnam Order of Battle, (New York, Galahad Books, 1886)pp148

[81] Russell, Lee E, Mendez, M. Albert, Grenada 1983, (London, England, Osprey Publishing Ltd., 1985),pp40

Bibliography

Cutler, Thomas J. *Brown Water, Black Beret*. Annapolis, Maryland: Naval Institute Press, 1988.

Linderer, Gary A. *The Eyes of the Eagle*. New York: Ivy Books,1991.

Linderer, Gary A. *Eyes Behind the Lines*. New York: Ivy Books, 1992.

Lyles, Kevin.*Vietnam: U.S. Uniforms in Colour Photographs*. London, England: Windrow & Greene., 1992.

Lyles, Kevin. *U.S. Infantry Vietnam*. Hong Kong: Concord Ltd., 1996

Renosa, Mark, *U.S. Combat Helmets of the 20th Century*. Schiffer Publishing, Ltd., 1997.

Rottman, Gordon L. *U.S. Army Rangers and LRRP Units, 1942-87*. London, England: Osprey Publishing Ltd., 1987.

Rottman, Gordon. *Panama, 1989-90*. London, England: Osprey Publishing Ltd., 1991.

Russell, Lee E. and Mendez, Albert. *Grenada 1983*. London, England: Osprey Publishing Ltd., 1985.

Smyth, Cecil B. *United States Coastal and River Forces in Vietnam*. American Society of Military Insignia Collectors, 1985.

Stanton, Shelby. *U.S. Uniforms of the Vietnam War*. Harrisburg, Pa: Stackpole Books., 1989.

Stanton, Shelby. *U.S. Uniforms of the Cold War, 1948-1973*. Mechanicsburg, Pa: Stackpole Books., 1994

Stanton, Shelby. *The Rise and Fall of an American Army. U.S. Ground Forces in Vietnam, 1965-1973*. Novato, Ca: Presidio Press.,1985.

Stanton, Shelby. *Vietnam Order of Battle*. New York: Galahand Books.,1986.

Stanton, Shelby. *Rangers at War*. New York: Ivy Books., 1992.

Tolson, Lieutenant General John J. *Airmobility in Vietnam*. New York: Arno Press., 1981.